T0275495

Latin America and the illusion of peace

David R. Mares

Latin America and the illusion of peace

David R. Mares

IISS The International Institute for Strategic Studies

The International Institute for Strategic Studies

Arundel House I 13–15 Arundel Street I Temple Place I London I WC2R 3DX I UK

First published May 2012 by **Routledge**
4 Park Square, Milton Park, Abingdon, Oxon, OX14 4RN

for **The International Institute for Strategic Studies**
Arundel House, 13–15 Arundel Street, Temple Place, London, WC2R 3DX, UK
www.iiss.org

Simultaneously published in the USA and Canada by **Routledge**
270 Madison Ave., New York, NY 10016

Routledge is an imprint of Taylor & Francis, an Informa Business

© 2012 The International Institute for Strategic Studies

DIRECTOR-GENERAL AND CHIEF EXECUTIVE Dr John Chipman
EDITOR Dr Nicholas Redman
ASSISTANT EDITOR Janis Lee
EDITORIAL Dr Jeffrey Mazo, Carolyn West, Antônio Sampaio, Dr Ayse Abdullah
COVER/PRODUCTION John Buck

The International Institute for Strategic Studies is an independent centre for research, information and debate on the problems of conflict, however caused, that have, or potentially have, an important military content. The Council and Staff of the Institute are international and its membership is drawn from almost 100 countries. The Institute is independent and it alone decides what activities to conduct. It owes no allegiance to any government, any group of governments or any political or other organisation. The IISS stresses rigorous research with a forward-looking policy orientation and places particular emphasis on bringing new perspectives to the strategic debate.

The Institute's publications are designed to meet the needs of a wider audience than its own membership and are available on subscription, by mail order and in good bookshops. Further details at www.iiss.org.

British Library Cataloguing in Publication Data
A catalogue record for this book is available from the British Library

Library of Congress Cataloging in Publication Data

ADELPHI series
ISSN 1944-5571

ADELPHI 429
ISBN 978-0-415-62706-1

Contents

ACKNOWLEDGEMENTS

I am grateful to the IISS editorial staff, both former and current, starting with James Lockhart Smith, who initially contacted me to propose this project and helped immeasurably with early conceptualisation. Nicholas Redman was most helpful in clarifying IISS's areas of interest and Janis Lee offered exceptional advice in the editing process. My research assistants Jaime Arredondo and Esteban Ferrero Botero were, as always, meticulous and reliable. All responsibility for views expressed herein is, nevertheless, mine alone.

ALBA	Bolivarian Alliance for the Peoples of our America
ARENA	Alianza Republicana Nacionalista
BNDES	Brazilian Development Bank
BOE	Barrels of oil equivalent
Caricom	Caribbean Community
CELAC	Community of Latin American and Caribbean States
CICTE	Inter-American Committee Against Terrorism
CSBM	Confidence- and security-building measure
CSN	South American Community of Nations
DEA	US Drug Enforcement Administration
DTO	Drug trafficking organisation
ELN	Ejército de Liberación Nacional
FARC	Fuerzas Armadas Revolucionarias de Colombia
FMLN	Frente Farabundo Martí para la Liberación Nacional
FSLN	Frente Sandinista de Liberación Nacional
HRW	Human Rights Watch
IACHR	Inter-American Commission on Human Rights
ICJ	International Court of Justice
IMF	International Monetary Fund
IRA	Irish Republican Army
LIO	Liberal international order
Mercosur	Common Market of the South
MID	Militarised inter-state dispute
MINUSTAH	UN Stabilization Mission in Haiti
MST	Landless Workers' Movement, Brazil

NGO	Non-governmental organisation
NOC	National oil company
OAS	Organisation of American States
SICA	Central American Integration System
SISFRON	Integrated Monitoring System of Borders, Brazil
UAV	Unmanned aerial vehicle
UNASUR	Union of South American Nations
UNSC	United Nations Security Council
WOLA	Washington Office on Latin America

In March 2008, Colombian armed forces crossed the border into Ecuador and attacked a guerrilla camp after, they claimed, the guerrillas opened fire on them. (It was subsequently revealed that Colombia had previously identified the location of the camp and had prepared an attack.[1]) Ecuador denounced the violation of its territory, broke off diplomatic ties and mobilised its military. Venezuela jumped into the fray, breaking relations with Colombia just a day after the raid, and ordering ten battalions (some 6,000 troops) to the border, while warning Colombia that violation of its territory would mean war. (Nicaragua also suspended relations with Colombia.) For a few days, as presidents Alvaro Uribe, Rafael Correa and Hugo Chávez traded threats and accusations, Latin Americans and many observers outside the region held their breath, until a reconciliation was brokered, symbolised by handshakes among the three leaders.[2]

It was not just the violation of a neighbour's sovereignty that caused alarm in this instance. Within 48 hours, two states had mobilised their forces in preparation for war, while an unapologetic Colombia insisted the raid, code-named *Operation Phoenix*, had been launched in response to the threat of terror. A third factor made the situation yet more complex: the crisis was triggered by Colombian forces chasing guerrillas, who constitute an internal threat to Colombia's democracy. Thus, both inter-state and domestic threats to security were at play. International and domestic events such as this suggest that Latin America is facing new and potentially destabilising challenges, both internally and externally, that are increasing national-security concerns and rekindling nationalist passions. These developments represent a threat to regional peace, democracy and prosperity, with concomitant negative impacts on the United States and the European Union.

Before we can mitigate the threat raised by militarised inter-state relations, it is necessary to explore the various ways in which military force can be employed short of war, as well as the decision-making process that produces militarisation of a disagreement. Conceptually, the militarisation of disputes is part of a strategy of inter-state bargaining. Military action, including war, does not occur out of the blue; there is a process of interaction that, at a particular juncture, results in one actor deciding that some level of use of military force would be advantageous in its dealings with a rival.

Since the use of military force is instrumental, we need to be aware of the issues around which tensions can develop to the level that military posturing is considered an appropriate option. That means considering not only the traditional issues concerning national boundaries, ideological competition and natural resources, but also new ones revolving around trans-border flows of people (illegal migrants, guerrillas, criminals, etc.) and goods (illegal drugs, weapons, etc.). In addition, we must understand the domestic motivations behind the decision to militarise. The decision to militarise almost always has popular support once it has been taken, so we need to understand why governments would consider it in their interests to do so, and why citizens would view such actions as legitimate. Finally, we should consider the range of options for defusing militarised conflict when it arises.

Latin American history warns against complacency. All militarised incidents have the potential to escalate into war; the initial level of militarisation offers no guide to the likely outcome.[3] Having been caught by surprise by the invasion that prompted the 1982 Malvinas/Falklands war, for example, the British government now takes Argentine declarations about sovereignty over the islands seriously. In the face of increasingly strident Argentine demands regarding the islands in 2010–11, then Defence Secretary Liam Fox said: 'We have Typhoons already stationed there. We have a very clear message that we have both the naval power if necessary, and certainly any [sic] intent to ensure that the Falkland Islands are kept free and their people enjoy the liberation we fought so hard for 30 years ago.'[4] The British defence community takes the potential for provocative Argentine action seriously enough to send its most advanced destroyer, HMS *Dauntless*, to the area and debated whether to send an aircraft carrier.[5]

The Latin American experience particularly warrants evaluation, since many analysts within the region and around the world appear to believe that inter-state military conflict has been eliminated from regional relations. The myth of Latin America as a region of peace has propagated itself to the extent that, each time the use of force gains global attention (e.g., Ecuador–Peru 1995 or Colombia–Ecuador 2008), analysts and the press express shock and disbelief. Yet, official uses of military force in inter-state relations are significantly more prevalent than most analysts are prepared to accept.

Inter-state conflict in Latin America

The international constraints on wars of obvious aggression and greed are sufficient to persuade Latin American countries, which are significantly immersed in the global economy and diplomatic world, that the costs of such military conflict would far outweigh the benefits. At the domestic level, Latin American publics do not sympathise with wars of conquest, despite their nationalistic tendencies. But low levels of militarised bargaining, such as verbal threats and displays of force, often meet with public support and a reticence on the part of international institutions to become involved. Thus low-level militarisation can reward the initiator and regional security institutions ironically create a 'moral hazard' promoting this risky behaviour.

Today the militarisation of conflict in Latin America is not about conquering neighbours, seizing large pieces of territory, or creating colonies or 'puppet' governments, as in the nineteenth and the first half of the twentieth century. The last such incident was Peru's war with Ecuador in 1941, which began on 5 July, with Ecuadorian forces ceasing to fight after three weeks and Peruvian troops occupying undisputed Ecuadorian territory until 11 February 1942. Under the treaty that ended the conflict, Ecuador ceded its claims on 40% of the disputed territory. Today's incidents of militarisation may be on a smaller scale, but they are nonetheless significant. For example, the Colombian military incursion into Ecuador in March 2008 resulted in military mobilisations in Ecuador and Venezuela, raising the spectre of war. Nicaragua still has a significant presence on its border with Costa Rica, following a mobilisation in 2010, which was ordered in spite of an International Court of Justice (ICJ) ruling that clarified the border along the San Juan River. In the sudden eruption of war between Ecuador and Peru in 1995, both navies were mobilised, along with bombers and helicopters and thousands of troops. The ensuing 34-day war cost some $250 million and caused the deaths of up to 400 people.[6] This rapid escalation reminds us that military posturing and threats can quickly develop into violent conflict, and that neither international nor domestic constraints are sufficient to keep Latin American countries (governments as well as citizens) from militarising disagreements they perceive to be important to national sovereignty, defence or security.

The militarised incidents that took place in the region from 2005 to 2011 are listed below in Table 1, alongside the corresponding level of military use or display. The Correlates of War project has usefully categorised the use of military force into five 'Hostility Levels': 1 = no use; 2 = threat; 3 = display; 4 = use < 1,000 battlefield related deaths; 5 = war. Militarised incidents between states do not include accidental cross-border crossings by military that are not protested by the country whose territory has been violated, nor military violence against criminals/ illegal migrants who cross into countries and are attacked by the forces there, unless that home country protests. The use of military force is of interest because of its potential, rather than actual, costs. All such incidents have the potential to escalate into war. There is, however, no pattern to the development of a militarised inter-state dispute (MID) or the evolution from an MID to war. More than one in ten (13%) of MIDs begin with a threat to use force, 38% initiate with a display of force and 49% erupt with outright use of force. The response to a MID does not vary by the hostility of the initial action: 47% of threats are responded to with threats, 59% of displays result in reciprocal displays, and 43% of the time use of force provokes a similar response.[7]

Sources of dispute in contemporary Latin America are varied. Even if countries no longer go to war to seize neighbours' territory, national boundaries remain contentious

Table 1 **Militarised Inter-state Disputes (2005–2011)**

Date	Countries	Incident	Hostility Level
Jan 2005	Venezuela; Colombia	Following revelations that Colombia paid bounty-hunters to kidnap a FARC leader from Caracas, Venezuela dispatches extra troops to the border.	3
Oct–Nov 2005	Costa Rica/ Nicaragua	Nicaraguan troop build-up on San Juan River; Nicaragua army commander visits posts to see if they need reinforcement; and coincident with his visit, the army parades tanks and troops in Managua.	2
2005–2007	Argentina/ Uruguay	During Argentine protest over pollution from Uruguayan paper mill on border, Argentine government tolerates blocking of international bridge and planting of hazards to navigation. In response Uruguay deploys troops.	3
Jan 2006	Colombia/ Ecuador	Colombia violates Ecuador's airspace.	3
April 2007	Nicaragua/ Costa Rica	Nicaraguan military detains Costa Rican leisure fishing boat which it claimed entered Nicaraguan waters; Costa Rican foreign minister protests.	4
Nov 2007	Venezuela/ Guyana	Venezuelan military blows up gold-mining dredges in area it claims (which is recognised internationally as Guyanese); Guyana government denounces attack.	
July 2007	Colombia/ Nicaragua	In response to dispute over sovereignty of San Andres, Colombia sends 1,200 troops to march on the island on Colombian Independence Day.	3
February 2008	Colombia/ Nicaragua	Colombia sends naval patrols to San Andres; Nicaraguan president says he'll complain to UN of harassment of fishermen.	3
March 2008	Colombia/ Ecuador	Colombia launches an air and ground offensive vs FARC camp across the Ecuadorian border. In protest, Ecuador withdraws its ambassador, protests aggression against Ecuadorian territory and dispatches troops to border.	4
March 2008	Colombia/ Venezuela	Protesting at Colombia's violation of Ecuador's territory, Venezuela expels Colombia's ambassador and entire diplomatic staff and announces deployment of ten battalions, fighter jets and tanks to border with Colombia. Chávez warns Colombia that a violation of Venezuela's territory would start a war in South America, and Chávez would respond with jet fighters.	3
October 2008	Paraguay/ Brazil	Paraguay complains to OAS that Brazilian military manoeuvres on the border are meant to intimidate it on bilateral issues.	3
Oct–Nov 2009	Belize/ Guatemala	Guatemala officially protests concerning Belizean construction of border posts and patrols.	2
November 2009	Venezuela/ Colombia	As response to Colombia–US base agreement, Chávez orders 15,000 troops to the border.	3

Table 1 **Militarised Inter-state Disputes (2005–2011)**

Date	Countries	Incident	Hostility Level
July 2010	Venezuela/ Colombia	Chávez orders troops to border to be on maximum alert after Uribe accuses him of supporting Colombian guerrillas.	3
July 2010	Nicaragua/ Colombia	Ortega warns Colombia that Nicaragua may respond militarily if the latter authorises oil concessions in disputed waters.	2
October 2010	Nicaragua/ Costa Rica	Nicaragua sends troops to disputed Isla Calero.	3
June 2011	Bolivia/Chile	Bolivia accuses Chile of abusing Bolivian soldiers who had wandered across the border with small arms.	2

Hostility Levels: 1 = no use; 2 = verbal threat; 3 = display; 4 = use < 1,000 battlefield related deaths; 5 = war

Source: Author database

issues between countries with the potential for militarisation. For example, Venezuela claims two-thirds of Guyana; Bolivia still demands a sovereign outlet to the sea through Chile; and Argentina claims the potentially hydrocarbon-rich Malvinas/ Falklands Islands under British control. Ideological competition in the region abated with the end of the Cold War, when countries embraced democracy and a consensus regarding liberal economic reforms in Latin America. But the 1998 election of Hugo Chávez in Venezuela, and his advocacy of a 'Socialism of the twenty-first century' at precisely the time that the poor and indigenous were becoming disenchanted with the distribution of benefits under the new economic growth strategies, rekindled the ideological fires. Cross-border ideological conflict can be especially severe, since it strikes at the legitimacy of a political system, and thus stimulates concern about a nation's sovereignty – that is, a government's mandate to make decisions in the name of its citizens. The boom in international commodity markets has brought inter-state competition over fisheries, hydrocarbons and other natural resources back onto the agenda in some parts of the region, while new issues of environmental damage and indigenous cultural survival are also gaining traction.

New sources of inter-state dispute have emerged as a result of the increased porosity of borders stemming from the globalisation of markets, the development of international law and innovations in communications technology. The international drug trade is taking on a regional dimension for Latin American countries as it exports increasing levels of violence in Mexico and Central America; previously, Latin American governments preferred to see the issue as one to be managed domestically by each country. *Operation Phoenix* dramatically threw the spotlight on growing concerns about the illicit trade in weapons and cross-border ties of insurgents to countries that either support or tolerate the rebellion.

Foreign private investment by Latin Americans investing in other Latin American countries has begun to feed resentment in some receiving countries that feel exploited by their traditional rivals, such as Paraguayans vis-à-vis Brazil or Bolivians regarding Chile. But the home countries of those investors may also view the recipient countries as unreliable when they nationalise foreign investment or limit business operations. When those investments were designed to integrate key sectors of the economies, the negative impact on confidence between neighbours can be significant.[8]

These varied sources of inter-state dispute are making themselves felt in increasingly destabilised domestic settings. There has been an explosion of violence stimulated by organised crime and urban gangs in many countries, which in turn creates a climate of fear among those living in the crossfire. Central governments and indigenous groups have clashed violently over the question of who controls the natural resources whose current and future exploitation could fuel economic growth. The distribution of economic gains has polarised politics in many countries, because high growth rates have not solved the problems of poverty. Empowered and frustrated citizens have taken to the streets, demanding rapid and dramatic resolution of grievances, and in numerous cases overthrowing governments incapable of meeting those demands. In several cases the military has stepped aside when initial attempts to control or disperse angry crowds produced violence (for example, Bolivia 2003), or have simply refused presidential orders to act (for example, Argentina 2001, Ecuador 2005).[9]

Responding to the domestic challenges and citizen demands, state power has increased as governments gain authority via constitutional reforms, legislative retreat and administrative fiat to diminish institutional constraints on their power in order to pursue perceived solutions. Along the way, many governments find themselves appealing to the military to complement the police in addressing internal security threats. These significant political changes in a number of countries raise concerns about the future of democracy; they also establish the norm that it is appropriate to use increasing levels of state power to address threats that have defied resolution by 'normal' means. The potential for carrying these lessons learned at the domestic level to relations with other countries must be considered.

In the context of regional and domestic tensions, the militaries of many nations are being significantly rebuilt after a period of restricted spending in the 1980s and 1990s, which was partly dictated by high levels of national debts and hyperinflation affecting many countries in Latin America. For example, Brazil was one of few Latin American countries to buck the trend for reining in defence expenditure (which rose from $1.6 billion to $1.77bn between 1986 and 1987, which it did on the back of rising growth and decreasing inflation). While inflation was being brought under control in most other Latin American countries at the same time, it remained high enough to put considerable constraints on military spending power.[10] The expenditures are not out of line with the size of national economies, particularly since the institutions were starved of resources for so long. Force modernisation, nevertheless, can contribute to a renewed rash of militarised inter-state disputes in the region as citizens and leaders call on their well-supplied militaries to demonstrate their relevance to the nation's defence of its interests.

Following the inter-state tensions and civil wars of the 1970s and 1980s, Latin American nations put in place a security architecture modelled on European systems, which was designed to prevent the recurrence of both militarised inter-state disputes and civil wars. Indeed, Latin America's security architecture is unique among developing countries in both its extent and breadth, since its institutions address both international and domestic threats. It has not, however, been up to the task of forestalling inter-state violence.

Latin America's security architecture

Since the wars of independence in the nineteenth century, Latin America's security context has essentially been a competitive one, in which deterrence and militarised bargaining have predominated among states that viewed each other as rivals rather than partners.[11] Resolution of the Central American civil wars in the 1980s, and the return to democracy throughout the region in the 1990s, generated expectations that the region could develop into a security community in which the use of military force among its members was inconceivable, much as in Western Europe. Latin American statesmen were not ignorant of the potential for conflict and actively promoted confidence- and security-building measures (CSBMs) throughout the hemisphere to facilitate the peaceful resolution of issues.

Latin America's security architecture, however, is overwhelmingly oriented towards addressing threats to democracy and those posed by non-state actors, rather than preventing the escalation of inter-state disputes. Two powerful reasons account for this focus. From the Latin American perspective, they had just emerged from decades of authoritarian governments, many of which had culminated in military dictatorships that were particularly disdainful of human rights (especially in Guatemala, El Salvador, Chile, Argentina and Uruguay). The fear of a return to that past made leftist groups that promoted violent revolution more appreciative of the benefits of what they had previously disparaged as 'bourgeois democracy'.[12] Moderate right-wing forces and the ideological centre had also learned the dangers to their own programmes posed by dictatorship. Citizens and politicians of Latin American countries were thus particularly sensitive to the potential overthrow of democracy and, for the first time in the region's history, set about building protection against this threat at the regional level.

The second factor influencing the emphasis on threats other than inter-state conflict is the US. Historically, the US has believed that the Western Hemisphere should emulate its political forms (for example, the Monroe Doctrine of 1823 proclaimed that republican forms of government would proliferate in the Americas if the monarchies of Europe would let the newly independent Spanish American colonies decide their own future) and economic systems. The so-called Washington Consensus in the 1990s about the appropriateness of democracy and liberal economics was, from the US perspective, Latin America's renewed recognition of that congruence between Latin America and the US. In terms of regional security, therefore, the US believes that Latin American countries should have the same view about threats as the US. The US does not feel threatened by Latin American countries that have no ties to US rivals outside the hemisphere, so it does not make sense to the US that Latin American countries should have rivalries amongst themselves. With the end of the Cold War, the US no longer worried that 'renegade' Latin American countries would align with US rivals outside the region and so its attention turned increasingly towards tackling the international trade in illegal drugs undertaken by non-state actors and the threats to democracy. From the US perspective, the happy result of this focus was that Latin American militaries would be re-directed to combat international crime (and after 11 September 2001, international terrorism), as well as assisting with international humanitarian missions and staying out of domestic politics.[13] Through military exchanges and training seminars, the Department of Defence believes that it is socialising Latin American militaries to adopt its own view of the region.

As a result of this security perspective generated among Latin Americans and promoted by the US, the security architecture relies heavily on a foundation whose core elements are democracy and economic integration. Democracy and economic integration are thus not only valuable in their own right, they have also become reified in the definition of regional security itself. The tendency is to expect that democratic consolidation and regional economic integration will simply take care of inter-state problems. In this framework, the role of the security structure is restricted to providing a forum for dialogue to lower tensions rather than to resolve problems. While there are theoretical arguments about the peaceful international impact of a community of democratic nations and economic interdependence, it would be unwise to ignore the contribution of interests in countries' decision to seek or accept greater integration.

The institutional structure that has been developed to support regional security is multidimensional in character and allows for the development of a flexible, regional response as the specific needs arise. As the Fifth Defence Ministerial Conference (Santiago, 2003) put it:

> the region has gradually advanced toward a complex security system made up of a network of new and old security institutions and regimes, both collective and cooperative, of hemispheric, regional, subregional and bilateral scope, which have in practice made up a new flexible security architecture.[14]

To buttress this security architecture, Latin American nations took a historic half-step away from their traditional emphasis on national sovereignty when the Organisation of American States' (OAS) 1991 General Assembly adopted the Santiago Commitment to Democracy and the Renewal of the Inter-American System. With this declaration, the member states singled out democratic standing as an indicator of a state's credibility in the search for security and articulated a desire to re-energise and refocus the OAS, involving it in CSBMs. The first Summit of the Americas (held in Miami, 1994) promoted the vision that CSBMs would defend democracy and enhance economic development.[15] While the Summits were designed independently of the OAS, the OAS became Secretariat of the Summit Process at the third Summit (Quebec City, 2001) and in 2001 adopted the Inter-American Democratic Charter to defend and promote democracy within the hemisphere.

Subregional organisations such as the Sistema de Integración Centroamericana (SICA, Central American Integration System) and the Union de Naciones Sudamericanas (UNASUR, Union of South American Nations) also address security issues. But while UNASUR helped mediate the 2008 dispute among Colombia, Ecuador and Venezuela, it did nothing to address the issues of FARC sanctuaries or access to resources in Venezuela or Ecuador. SICA has addressed the drug trade as a threat to security,[16] but does not take on the issue of military posturing and threats by one member-state against another, as in the ongoing situation between Nicaragua and Costa Rica.

The effectiveness of the security architecture in dissuading states from militarising their disputes has been handicapped by a number of factors. There is no coherent regional vision of security which integrates the inter-state security threats. In addition, the Declaration on Security in the Americas 'securitises' a number of other important problems such as organised crime and urban gangs. Treating such issues as security threats implies a military solution to problems which militaries can do little to help solve; expansion of the role of the military to address such problems also undermines citizen security, civilian control of the military and ultimately, perhaps even democracy. Other than a military coup, there is no agreement among countries as to the circumstances that constitute a threat to democracy

The regional security architecture is consistent with a robust liberal democratic regional context; unfortunately, many Latin American democracies are either non-liberal or have weak Liberal institutions. For example, in Venezuela the government has adopted an increasingly flexible definition of the rule of law.[17] Legislatures in many countries operate with the opposition forcibly excluded (such as when the Bolivian Constituent Assembly passed a draft of the new constitution in 2007).[18] Elections themselves are extremely problematic (for example, the Nicaraguan municipal elections of 2008 were criticised by international observers).[19] In addition, newly elected members of parliament have found their powers severely constrained or even eliminated by the government (such as the case of opposition candidates who won governorships in Venezuela's 2008 election, who found their powers largely turned over to newly created military districts, and the newly elected Congress in 2010 was pre-empted by the outgoing Congress, which granted President Chávez the right to rule by decree for 18 months).[20] Consequently, the peace-enhancing potential of the regional security architecture is significantly hampered in Latin America.

In addition, the reliance of the security architecture on economic integration is problematic because economic integration processes have stagnated throughout the region after a promising start in the 1990s. This has resulted from increased economic nationalism in some states (such as Bolivia and Argentina) and the political costs of integration. As integration proceeds, it increasingly requires that national economic policies become more complementary, a point that has been slow to dawn upon leaders in the eurozone countries since 2008. This requirement for complementarity raises the political costs of integration, as governments would have to force domestic actors to forgo some monopoly profits or subsidies. Mercosur, created in 1991, has essentially not progressed beyond being a customs union among Argentina, Brazil, Uruguay and Paraguay, despite the associate status of Chile and Bolivia.[21] Central American integration is becoming concentrated among the three northern nations of Guatemala, Honduras and El Salvador, with Nicaragua, Costa Rica and Panama largely opting out of deeper integration, preferring instead to pursue options outside Central America.[22] The US-inspired Free Trade Association of the Americas is dead and the Alianza Bolivariana para los Pueblos de Nuestra América (Bolivarian Alliance for the Peoples of Our America, or ALBA), set up by Chávez in 2004, is going nowhere either. Bilateral trade agreements have proliferated among Latin American countries, but the boom in trade between Colombia and Venezuela up to 2008 and its subsequent decline by approximately one-third from

2008 to 2011 illustrates that politics can still trump economic logic in bilateral-integration schemes. Consequently, integration is too limited to produce the expected peace; therefore, relying on integration as a means to mitigate conflict weakens the ability of the regional security architecture to deter or effectively manage conflict.

Significance of Latin American conflict

The negative fallout from renewed conflict in Latin America threatens Latin Americans and non-Latin Americans. The supply of natural resources, including oil and natural gas, could be affected, resulting in reduced Latin American supplies to local, regional and global markets. This could occur alongside increased demand from a growing Latin America on those reduced supplies, leading initially to price spikes locally as neighbours seek to develop the infrastructure and contacts to substitute regional sources with global ones. Constrained supplies for export from Latin American producers (particularly Venezuela, which now has more oil reserves than Saudi Arabia; Brazil, with its immense offshore hydrocarbon reserves; and Argentina, which is estimated to have the-third largest known shale gas reserves in the world[23]) would also create a situation that contrasts significantly with projections that the global impact of the Middle East may be in decline.[24] Diminished state capacity because of internal and external conflict would also provide more opportunities for organised crime to prosper, and perhaps increase its global reach in illicit goods and links to terrorism. Economic refugees from a number of Latin American countries are already a contentious issue for the US, Spain and within Latin America; a new wave of domestic and regional insecurity would further undermine personal security and economic opportunities, stimulating even more out-migration at a time when traditional receiving countries are less willing to deal cooperatively with it. Economic dislocation would mean slower economic growth in the region, and thus less international trade, threats to existing investments and diminished opportunities for future investment, both regional and international.

We ignore the signs of potential militarised conflict in Latin America at our peril. Boundary disagreements and ideological competition have not disappeared. The resurgence of populism and nationalism threaten the latest wave of democracy and the foundations of economic growth. The modernisation of the military, while necessary, comes at a time when those increased capabilities have the potential to further destabilise bilateral relations where inter-state tensions have not been resolved. As it becomes clear that the efforts of the last two decades to build regional peace and prosperity upon a combination of CSBMs and liberal democracy have fallen significantly short of meeting today's challenges, it is imperative that we undertake a review of the internal and international conflicts in order to understand the options for preventing or mitigating violent inter-state conflict and which might be most effective in forestalling violent confrontation.

©IISS

UNITED STATES

Atlantic Ocean

THE BAHAMAS

MEXICO   Havana ■

CUBA

Mexico City ■   BELIZE   JAMAICA   HAITI   DOMINICAN REPUBLIC

Belmopan   Kingston ■   Port-au-   Santo Domingo ■

GUATEMALA ■   Tegucigalpa   Prince

Guatemala City ■   HONDURAS

EL SALVADOR   NICARAGUA

San Salvador ■   COSTA RICA   TRINIDAD & TOBAGO

Managua ■   Panama   Caracas ■   Georgetown ■

San Jose ■   City ■   VENEZUELA   Paramaribo ■

PANAMA   ■ Bogota   GUYANA   SURINAM   Cayenne ■

COLOMBIA   FRENCH GUYANA

Quito ■

ECUADOR

PERU   B R A Z I L

■ Lima

La Paz   ■ Brasilia

■   BOLIVIA

PARAGUAY

Asuncion ■

CHILE

URUGUAY

Santiago ■   Buenos Aires ■ ■ Montevideo

ARGENTINA

Pacific Ocean

Falkland Islands (UK)

Miles   1,000   South Georgia (UK)

Kilometres   1,500

CHAPTER ONE

Sources of conflict

Inter-state relations in Latin America have been a source of tension since independence, despite historical and cultural ties and the shared belief of many within and outside the region that the common experience of exploitation by the world powers should provide a common bond. Verbal threats and displays and the use of force have occurred far more often than is generally perceived by Latin Americans as well as by those outside the region. Although there has been no major war in the region since the Chaco War (1932–35), violent conflict did erupt into wars throughout the twentieth century (Peru–Ecuador 1941, El Salvador–Honduras 1969, Argentina–United Kingdom 1982 and Ecuador–Peru 1995). There have also been serious war scares (the San Juan River dispute between Nicaragua and Costa Rica, which last flared up in 2010; Peru/Bolivia–Chile in 1977, over a possible Bolivian outlet through the sea via territory Chile conquered from Peru; the Beagle conflict between Argentina and Chile in 1978 over three islands; and operations to bring down the Sandinista government in Nicaragua, carried out by US-backed counter-revolutionaries (Nicaraguan contras) from Honduran territory, 1982).[1] The US has also launched direct invasions in the hemisphere, for example, in the Dominican Republic in 1965, Grenada in 1983 and Panama in 1989; and covert military operations, such as the US-sponsored coup in Guatemala in 1954 and the failed US-proxy invasion of Cuba in 1961.

While almost all of the incidents involving the US (Honduras–Nicaragua, the Dominican Republic, Grenada, Guatemala and Cuba) were related in some way to the Cold War, other events – particularly those related to intra-Latin American conflicts – were not. Indeed, the end of the bipolar distribution of world power did not produce peace and understanding among Latin American nations. Historical grievances as well as new issues stimulate conflict in the region, with the potential that one or both sides will see the use of force as an acceptable tool for settling their differences.

Boundary disputes as well as ideological rivalries (which contest the grounds upon which a government can claim the legitimacy to govern) constitute the core elements underlying the potential for inter-state conflict in the region. In addition to their direct impacts, these core sources of conflict are also at play in controversies over trade in energy and other natural resources. Cooperation has the potential to produce dependency and to sharpen a sense of exploitation felt by the state that receives energy from a neighbour. Tensions are also produced by the increasing porosity of borders. But none of these can be viewed in isolation. The internal context is crucial to building an understanding of why governments may seek to resolve, or refocus attention on, these significant inter-state disagreements.

Inter-state controversies
Boundary disputes
Scores of boundary disputes in Latin America have arisen and been resolved throughout its history. These disputes have

entailed physical and jurisdictional claims on land, water or airspace. Also falling into this category are disagreements over who makes the rules governing the behaviour of the civilian and military vessels of other countries within the territorial sea and airspace claimed by the coastal state. These disputes over sovereignty have produced displays of force and seizures of vessels that have developed and could again develop into extremely tense scenarios, if the long-standing and new factors that exacerbate inter-state conflict are not well managed.

Some of the solutions to boundary disputes were imposed violently, while others were peacefully negotiated at the bilateral or multilateral level. Many of the disagreements were even submitted to binding arbitration and, most of the time, the arbiter's decision was accepted by both parties. Between 2000 and 2011 seven inter-state disputes of varying types were resolved, with another five in an active process towards resolution (see Appendix Three). Three boundary disputes are currently at various stages of International Court of Justice processes (between Nicaragua and Colombia over the islands of San Andreas and Providencia; a maritime dispute between Peru and Chile; and the Isla Calero dispute between Costa Rica and Nicaragua). The OAS is mediating another process dealing with a border dispute between Guatemala and Belize.

Boundaries continue to be challenged, as can be seen in Appendix Two. In 2005 Chile was surprised when, after the final resolution of their land-based disagreements, Peru suddenly declared that their maritime boundaries were in dispute. Ecuador, seeing the dispute with Chile, demanded clarification of Peru's position on their shared maritime boundary. In May 2011, the Chileans learned that the Peruvians had accepted a division with Ecuador based largely on the same criteria that Peru had previously rejected with Chile.[2] Bolivia is concerned that years of bilateral discussions with Chile will not lead to a sovereign outlet to the sea and has threatened to take its claim to the ICJ, unless significant progress is made towards that goal.[3] Although Chile had accepted the submission of the dispute with Peru to the ICJ, in light of Ecuador's achievement in its dispute with Peru without ICJ intervention and the existence of a peace treaty with Bolivia that does not grant it a sovereign access to the sea, Chile refuses to be pressured by Bolivia and resentment on both sides is growing. In another matter, international judgments have by no means been the final word. The 2003 ruling by the ICJ to resolve the Honduras–El Salvador dispute in the Gulf of Fonseca inadvertently created a new controversy, by failing to specify which country had sovereignty over the tiny Isla de Conejo; both parties claim the island. To return to the aforementioned San Juan River dispute, which was subject to an ICJ ruling confirming Nicaraguan sovereignty over the river that separates that country from Costa Rica, Nicaragua has asserted claims to a portion of the Isla Calero previously considered Costa Rican, and dispatched troops to defend the dredging of a channel there. Costa Rica protested that this was a breach of its sovereignty, moved police forces to the border and appealed to the OAS for support.

The high price of energy has turned maritime boundaries into a much larger issue than fisheries, as countries scramble to sign contracts with international oil companies to explore for fossil fuels in disputed territories. Venezuela used force in 1999 to assert its claims to the the natural-gas resources in the seas between it and Trinidad and Tobago; it then entered into negotiations with the island nation in 2003 and finally signed an agreement in 2010 over the division of the resources. Some Costa Rican analysts believe that Nicaragua's expectations regarding potential hydrocarbon deposits off its Gulf coast seem to stimulate it to deal forcefully with Costa

Rica, since it is waiting for an ICJ ruling on maritime boundaries with Colombia that it might lose and to whom it made
a militarised threat in 2010.[4] In early 2010, as a result of the
renewed interest in oil exploration in the area, Argentina began
demanding that financial and commercial activity between
the mainland and the disputed Falkland/Malvinas Islands
recognise Argentine sovereignty over the islands. Subsequent
exploration in 2011, which suggested promising, though risky
and expensive, reserves, combined with the 30th anniversary
of the Falklands/Malvinas War to produce nationalist rhetoric
from Argentine leaders, violent street demonstrations against
the British Embassy in Buenos Aires, and a growing debate in
the UK concerning what is militarily necessary to deter another
Argentine seizure of the islands.

Political–ideological disputes

The nineteenth century was dominated by a split between
liberals and positivists, on the one hand, and conservatives
and Catholics on the other, while the twentieth century saw
opposition between communist and liberal ideologies, with
fascism contributing to ideological tensions from the 1920s
into the 1950s. The end of the Cold War and re-democratisa-
tion in Latin America opened up space for a wider spectrum
of political and ideological viewpoints to be openly articulated
domestically and regionally. Initially, this space was occupied not only by parties from the political centre but also by
the 'reformed' left and right, both eschewing victory through
force and accepting the slower and more halting path of liberal
democracy. Former guerrillas from the Frente Farabundo Martí
para la Liberación Nacional (FMLN) on the left and the death-
squad-linked Alianza Republicana Nacionalista (ARENA)
on the right competed for office in El Salvador; Sandinistas
competed against Contras in Nicaragua; members of Salvador

Allende's coalition formed part of the governing Concertación alliance in Chile; and the ex-dictator General Hugo Banzer became a respected senator and was then democratically elected as president in Bolivia.

The democratic opening was deeper and more effective in this third wave of democratisation than in prior efforts in the early and mid-twentieth century in Latin America. Governments generally undertook measures to broaden and deepen political participation as well as institute neo-liberal economic reforms. The implications for domestic politics of the failures of these economic reforms to significantly improve the plight of the poor and indigenous at the same time these formerly marginal sectors of society were experiencing greater political empowerment will be examined in the next section. Here we want to examine the impact of these failures on regional relations through their impact on ideology.

Despite the media depiction of a 'pink tide' (in contrast to the 'red' of communism) moving the region leftward, the shift has been neither linear nor consistent across the region. Alan Garcia in Peru (1985–1990) came to power with a traditional leftist programme, the implementation of which brought the country to economic and political collapse, followed by a rapid expansion of the Sendero Luminoso guerrilla movement. These failures made possible Alberto Fujimori's semi-authoritarian and pro-market reign from 1990–2000. The Socialist Party in Chile and Fernando Henrique Cardoso in Brazil were the first successful instances in those countries of a democratically elected left in the 1990s, but they achieved office in alliance with centrist political forces and focused on using public policy to promote efficient market reforms, while mitigating their negative social impacts. Venezuela's Hugo Chávez in 1998 became the first of a new group of candidates to come to office specifically denouncing the reformist path to development and poverty reduction. When candidates on the left in other countries also achieved public office on platforms critiquing the centre, the media became infatuated with the notion of the pink tide.

The concept, however, distorts our understanding of the political and ideological tensions that have arisen in the region since 1998. Rather than a division into pink leftists and neo-liberals of the centre-right, political forces in the region are more usefully broken down into five groups. The pink left is actually comprised of a pragmatic left (Dilma Rousseff in Brazil, José Mújica in Uruguay, Fernando Lugo in Paraguay and Mauricio Funes in El Salvador) and a new populist left. The populist left, which demands results more quickly than the pragmatic left, includes Chávez in Venezuela, Hugo Morales in Bolivia, Daniel Ortega in Nicaragua, Rafael Correa in Ecuador, Manuel Zelaya until his overthrow in June 2009 in Honduras, and Christina Fernández de Kirchner in Argentina. Even further to the left are groups that are more philosophically in tune with anarchist-like demands for local control by workers, peasants, women and indigenous peoples, who are willing to engage in violent civil disobedience to achieve it (for example, Vice President Alvaro Garcia Linera in Bolivia, as well as some indigenous groups in Bolivia, Ecuador, Peru, Mexico and Chile). The centre-right is represented by the neo-liberals (for example, Juan Manuel Santos in Colombia, Felipe Calderón in Mexico, Sebastian Piñera in Chile, Ricardo Martinelli of Panama, Laura Chinchilla in Costa Rica, Porfirio Lobo in Honduras and the recent ex-President Alan García in Peru – the latter having moved right from his earlier days). There is also a growing movement on the ultra-right (for example, the autonomy movement in eastern Bolivia, and some of the opposition in Venezuela and Honduras) who, in an ominous echo of the past, believe that democracy has to be temporarily set aside in order to be 'saved'.[5] And of course, governments themselves are usually created with cross-party alliances that span a spectrum of views (for example, in Chile and Brazil) or have a range of views within the governing party (for example, Ecuador and Mexico).

The two extreme political forces on the left and the right incorporate the use of violence on the legal margins (for example, during public demonstrations) in their political programmes, while the other three political forces are resorting to the use of police and military more quickly, albeit within the limits of the law (though it must be recogniseed that Colombia and Brazil have long been accused of going beyond the law to deal with political and economic opponents in the former and gangs in the latter). Although there are anti-democratic movements on the left (FARC in Colombia, Sendero Luminoso in Peru, some anarchists in Chile) and on the right (paramilitaries in Colombia and Guatemala), they are not important political forces at this time.

As it has so often in Latin America, ideology is contributing once again to increased inter-state tension and exacerbating inter-state conflict in multiple ways. The populists in particular have been prone to meddle in their neighbours' politics either through rhetoric or money (for example, Chávez' characterisation of political leaders opposed to his favoured candidates in other nations as puppets of US imperialism and his provision of subsidised fuel to populist mayors in Central America; Ortega's rhetoric about his 'brothers' in the FARC; and Morales's accusations against García's policies in Peru, which even provoked a recall of the Peruvian ambassador).

There is also concern about violence increasingly becoming acceptable to those on the furthest ends of the political spectrum. For example, Colombia has accused Chávez of providing material support to the FARC, an accusation substantiated in the computer files seized during *Operation Phoenix*.[6] On the extreme right, individuals have been arrested for plotting to assassinate President Morales in Bolivia, and there have been several instances of violence directed against the government and its supporters in the right-dominated eastern department of Pando. Ideological tensions also lead populists to fear intervention by proxies of the US, such as when Chávez called for the region to 'prepare for war' in the wake of Colombia's agreement to share its military bases with the US. But ideological tensions are not just expressed at the bilateral level. Chávez has declared his willingness to send Venezuelan forces to Bolivia to protect the Morales government, or against Colombia to defend Ecuador.

Chávez has even gone as far as to court states that openly express enmity towards the US. Amid overtures that altered the diplomatic context for Latin America, Chávez met the Iranian president in October 2010 to discuss building ties between the nations, and has approved new visa-free flight connections between Caracas and Tehran, which could provide conduits for the covert transfer of money and individuals.[7] The 2012 presidential election campaign has been marked by anti-Semitic remarks about his opponent, Henrique Capriles Radonski, who is the son of Jewish immigrants. Morales, Correa and Ortega have developed their own warm relations with the Iranian government. Brazil, which is trying to play a larger role in world politics, invited first the Israeli government and subsequently Iran for meetings with President Lula, further legitimating Ahmadinejad in the region and provoking critical comments from the US.[8] When Bolivia hosted Iranian Defense Minister Ahmad Vahidi at a military ceremony, Argentina protested that Vahidi has been accused of giving the order to bomb a Jewish cultural centre in Buenos Aires in 1994 and there is an Interpol warrant for his arrest. Bolivia claimed to be ignorant of these accusations, expelled the diplomat and patched up relations with the Argentine government.[9] In late 2011, a covert US government operation led to the arrest of an Iranian and charges against the Iranian Revolutionary Guards' Quds Force for attempting to assassinate the Saudi Ambassador to the US, which was allegedly to be arranged by the Mexican drug-trafficking organisation Los Zetas.[10] Iran's diplomatic offensive has succeeded in creating a more visible role for itself in the hemisphere, adding fuel to the ideological tensions in the Western Hemisphere.[11]

Energy and natural resources
Energy and natural resources as a source of inter-state tension in Latin America are not new phenomena, but their contribution is growing as Latin American capital flows across borders within the region and countries begin to depend more on each other for these resources. The two core factors underlying inter-state controversies over energy and natural resources are boundary disputes and ideological differences. Boundary disputes affect claims to natural resources, whether hydro-carbons or the flows of scarce water resources. Ideological differences that impact inter-state relations arise about the proper distribution of rents (that is, profits greater than can be obtained in a competitive market) associated with natural resources, the priorities for their use (domestic consumption or export market, or industrial crops versus food-crops) and dependency. Trade issues and investment flows also have an impact on inter-state controversies over energy and natural resources.

The erroneous expectation of large oil reserves in the Chaco was one of the precipitating factors in Bolivia's decision to go to war in the 1930s against Paraguay. The attraction of oil was a factor, though a minor one, in the Argentine decision to occupy the Falklands/Malvinas Islands in 1982, thus precipitating war with the UK. Despite suffering a military defeat in this campaign, Argentina still has not renounced its claims and now the start of exploration for oil and gas by British-licensed firms is generating increasing tensions.[12] Venezuela has displayed not only naval power but also air-force over-flights in the Gulf of Venezuela, where boundaries with Colombia are in dispute; the border disputes in gas-rich waters between Venezuela and Trinidad and Tobago even resulted in Venezuelan patrol boats firing on a production platform before the two countries came to an agreement on sharing the gas in 2007.[13] Discoveries of significant offshore oil and gas reserves after 2007 will reportedly take Brazil from 11th in the global oil-producer rankings, at around 100,000 barrels per day, to the world's fifth-largest producer or higher by 2020, with 4.9 million barrels per day from the pre-salt layer alone.[14] This prospect has led it to seek to significantly increase the deterrent and defensive capabilities of its navy and air force to protect those resources. Brazil's defence spending rose by 35% in nominal terms between 2008 and 2011, with around a fifth of resources channelled towards equipment procurement.[15]

Even when ownership of hydrocarbons is not contested, they can still contribute to inter-state tensions. Latin American national oil companies (NOCs) and private firms are investing in the exploration, production, transportation and marketing of hydrocarbons in other countries. The rise in resource nationalism in some producing countries has resulted in the seizure of property in Bolivia and Ecuador and forced contract renegotiations affecting Brazilian and Argentine investors. The Brazilian government negotiated a settlement with Bolivia, but its NOC Petrobras left Ecuador in 2010 rather than accept contract renegotiations. The Brazilian government used a massive military display of force on the border with Paraguay to signal its concern over the seizure of Brazilian-owned farms by landless Paraguayans and the general Paraguayan discontent with the energy relationship at Itaipu (see below).

Trade in hydrocarbons was supposed to stimulate regional economic integration and promote cooperation. But the trade has not transcended the sources of conflict. Chile, a historical rival of Argentina with whom it was on the verge of war as recently as 1978, took a major step in 1994 in deciding to become heavily dependent upon Argentine natural gas for its power generation. The Chilean government believed the benefits would include not only lower prices and lower pollution, but also a new cooperative relationship with its neighbour. Both countries benefitted and were duly cited as a prime example of the advantages of trade, particularly in energy. In 2004, however, Argentina responded to internal economic crises by cutting exports of natural gas to Chile, which then experienced dramatic power shortages. After the gas dispute, despite Argentina's significant demilitarisation and success in subordinating the military to civilian control, Chileans once again perceive Argentina as the major external threat to their country: in 1991, 46% of Chileans believed it possible that Argentina could attack the country; in 2007 that figure had risen to 53.7%.[16]

The negative fallout of energy trade does not just affect the consuming nations. Bolivians have had a difficult time dealing with their status as exporters of natural gas. In the 1970s Bolivia and Argentina signed a gas deal, but subsequently Argentina discovered its own large gas reserves; Bolivians protested as Argentina sought a decrease in both the quantity and price of gas imports from Bolivia. In another intra-Latin American flash-point, in 2003 the Bolivian government of Gonzalo Sánchez de Lozada decided to export natural gas to Mexico and the US through Chile; this route was extremely controversial in part because of a history of ill-feeling dating back to the nineteenth century, when Chile took territory from Bolivia in the War of the Pacific.[17] Faced with massive demonstrations that blocked highways and destroyed property, the government ordered the army to break the blockade. In the ensuing violence, scores of people died. Sanchez de Lozada suspended the natural-gas export project, resigned and fled to the US, which refuses to extradite him to Bolivia for trial. Under the Morales government, Bolivia has not only nationalised all gas fields, but has demanded higher prices for gas already contracted; Argentina accepted the upward price revisions, but Brazil (its largest client) insisted on its contracted price, leaving many Bolivians feeling exploited. Unfortunately for Bolivia, its three natural markets (Brazil, Chile and Argentina) have developed the ability to import liquified natural gas from outside the region. In addition, Brazil has discovered large oil and gas reserves offshore and Argentina has significant reserves of shale gas. The fall in price of Bolivian gas and export volumes that will likely develop as a result may leave the Bolivians feeling abused by their neighbours once again.

Hydrocarbons are not the only natural resources that provoke inter-state tensions. Chilean and Brazilian investments in mining in Bolivia and Peru have also generated controversy with resource nationalists. In Ecuador, indigenous movements protested at a mining law passed by the Correa government, leading to violent clashes; Correa retreated, calling for negotiations, but the indigenous insist that their Amazonian regions will remain mining-free territories, despite the legally sanctioned presence of multinational mining companies.[18] It is important to note that this is an instance of the increasingly prevalent phenomenon of a populist leftist government being outflanked on the left by more radical grassroots elements. Other natural-resource concerns also play a role. Colombia celebrated its Independence Day in 2007 with President Alvaro Uribe reviewing a large military parade on the island of San Andres, whose maritime delimitation, and thus the rights to an exclusive economic zone under the international Law of the Sea Treaty, is contested with Nicaragua.[19] And a new maritime boundary dispute in fishing-rich waters developed between Peru and Chile in 2005 when Peru adopted a law that unilaterally redrew its boundary with Chile. Ill feeling was further fuelled by alleged spying by the Chilean military.[20]

Brazil finds its interests at risk in these non-hydrocarbon natural-resource controversies because its national interests in mining, agriculture and hydropower conflict not only with local resource-nationalism, but also with global interests in protecting the environment and indigenous peoples. Brazil recognises this tension and has repeatedly asserted its intention to defend its sovereign control over the Amazon, building roads into the region and developing a radar system to observe activity there. The government has supported expanding the ability of the armed forces to defend its vast territory in the Amazon and that is one of its rationales for the current purchases of sophisticated arms (for more detail on this, see Chapter Three).

Brazil and Paraguay have a number of disagreements revolving around the use of natural resources (as well as the use of the Brazilian currency, flag, language, and school curriculum in the Paraguayan border regions). Brazilians residing in Paraguay have turned the country into the world's fourth-largest producer of soybeans with their highly mechanised agribusiness model, but in the process have displaced Paraguayan peasants and traditional crops. The land-reform movement in Paraguay specifically targets these vast Brazilian-owned soybean farms and violent confrontations have occurred. Another source of tension for decades between Brazil and Paraguay has been the Itaipu power complex. Under the

1973 agreement for building the dam and power plants, each country received half of the power generated, but was required to sell to the other at cost any electricity not used nationally. Paraguay uses less than 10% of its share and over time came to see the requirement to sell 90% to Brazil at cost as one more instance of Brazilian exploitation. In 2009, the two governments finally renegotiated the contract, which was given final approval in May 2011. This contract will give Paraguay price increases of 200% as well as Brazilian investments in infrastructure to the tune of US$450 million.[21]

The Brazilian government has already brought its military to bear on some of these disputes. To protect Brazilian property and interests at Itaipu, for example, the Brazilian government pressured its Paraguayan counterpart by sending troops to the border. On 17 October 2008, in *Operation Southern Border II*, 10,000 Brazilian troops used planes, tanks, ships, and live munitions in exercises that included a mock occupation of the Itaipu Dam and rescue of Brazilian citizens. General José Elito Carvalho Siquiera, chief of the Southern Military Command, told the Brazilian press: 'The time for hiding things is over. Today we have to demonstrate that we are a leader, and it is important that our neighbours understand this. We cannot continue to avoid exercising and demonstrating that we are strong, that we are present, and we have the capacity to confront any threat.' The general also declared that any interference with the Itaipu hydroelectric complex, even by a social movement, would be a national-security issue that merited military involvement. The Brazilian foreign minister took a position as well, noting that the Paraguayan government had to control the 'excesses' being committed by Paraguayans against Brazilians residing in Paraguay. The Lugo government understood that it was being pressured and complained about Brazilian behaviour at a meeting of the OAS Permanent Assembly.[22]

The significant ownership and use of agricultural land by citizens of other countries raises ideological issues concerning food security, land reform, and anti-market perspectives. These issues go far beyond intra-Latin American relations, because most multinational corporations involved in production and trade of agricultural products are foreign-owned and -based; for example, both Argentina and Paraguay have limited foreign ownership of agricultural land, and Brazil is debating such legislation.[23] But the issue does come up within Latin America, particularly with respect to soybeans, as in the Paraguayan case. In Uruguay, Argentines control half the soybean production, while Brazilians dominate in Uruguay's rice production (the country's largest export crop) and the meat industry. Resource nationalists in Uruguay are concerned about both the dependency on foreign capital and the growing redirection of farmland for export crops.[24] In Bolivia, protests have forced the government to limit exports of cooking oil.[25]

Environmental concerns are also driving a wedge between Latin American states. The huge Gasbol pipeline to transport Bolivian gas across the Bolivian Amazon to Brazilian markets has caused damage to the environment and indigenous cultures, despite assurances to the contrary.[26] Elsewhere, although the ICJ ruled in 2010 in favour of Uruguay's development of a paper mill on the river that separates the two countries, Argentines continued to demonstrate, fearing that the mill could contaminate the common waters. In the autumn of 2009, indigenous groups protested at the San Francisco hydroelectric dam project undertaken in the Ecuadorian Amazon by the Brazilian company Odebrecht Construction. Under pressure from the far left, the Correa government responded by imposing a lien on the company's properties in Ecuador and contested the legality of a US$243m loan provided by the Brazilian National Development Bank (BNDES) for the project, including it among the foreign debt repudiated by the Ecuadorian government. Brazil responded by recalling its ambassador.[27]

Increasing porosity of borders

Borders used to provide citizens and governments with a sense of control over their fate and re-enforced a sense of national identity. But today borders are increasingly porous, because of the globalisation of markets, international laws concerning human rights, and technological innovations that make communication across national borders easy and instantaneous. While these particular 'border-penetrating' factors are generally regarded as positive, they do challenge traditional notions of what it means to be a sovereign nation. But borders are also penetrated by the flow of people and goods perceived to constitute threats, thus generating demands for mitigation by citizens and states perceiving themselves to be victims.

One of the 'new' issues confronting the region is the increased power of organised crime and its consequent ability to affect more citizens in their daily lives. Crime which crosses borders raises the potential for scapegoating a neighbour, particularly if boundary and ideological disputes already exist between the countries. If transnational crime creates enough concern among citizens, it can destabilise international relationships.

The illegal drug trade is an important issue, but Latin American countries reject the notion of an international drug war, preferring to focus on internal methods for crime fighting. Brazil is certainly affected by the flows of cocaine from Colombia and marijuana from Paraguay (the second-largest producer of cannabis in the world), but it prefers to keep the issue off the inter-state agenda. Colombian cocaine production stimulates the growth of illegal coca cultivation in Bolivia and Peru, and trafficking routes traverse Central America, Ecuador, Venezuela and even non-neighbouring Chile and Mexico.

Guatemala's President Otto Pérez Molina (a retired general) has proposed legalising drugs, Mexico's Felipe Calderón wants to discuss the topic, and Colombia's Juan Manuel Santos wants the topic discussed at the 2012 Summit of the Americas, which was due to be hosted by his country as this book went to press. Nevertheless, all Latin American countries, except Colombia, address the drug trade as a crime issue to be handled according to each country's autonomously determined domestic laws.

The US, however, insists that drugs constitute a national-security issue requiring highly punitive international and national responses, thereby setting a basis for conflict between the US and Latin America, and among Latin American countries. The US has sanctioned both Venezuela and Bolivia for not adhering to US prescriptions for tackling the drug trade, but given the Latin American perspective and the failure of those prescriptions to make a significant dent in the trade, such sanctions are perceived simply as political tools to use against ideological rivals. US strategy also turns the drug trade into an inter-state issue within Latin America. Ecuador has elevated to the ICJ its concern about the cross-border implications of herbicidal spraying. In addition, the US–Colombian approach to he FARC (which combines elements of counter-insurgency, anti-drug and anti-terrorism strategies) pushes the guerrillas across the Ecuadorian, Venezuelan and Panamanian borders in search of refuge. Colombia and the US have accused Ecuador and Venezuela of harbouring FARC, while Ecuador and Venezuela accuse Colombia and its ally of purposely not patrolling the Colombian side of the border to prevent rebels from leaving their country of origin. The 2008 Colombian decision to attack FARC in Ecuador and the US support for the decision turned the combined issue of drugs, FARC and terrorism into potentially the most dangerous trigger to significant inter-state military conflict in the region (see Chapter Three).

The illegal trade in arms feeds insurgents, organised crime and urban gangs, often generating cross-border tensions, especially when state involvement is perceived. When Colombia charged that weapons they had recovered from FARC were supplied by Venezuela, Chávez responded by recalling the Venezuelan ambassador from Colombia and freezing relations between the nations once again. Colombia further alleged that the weapons included three Swedish AT-4 rocket launchers sold by Sweden to the Venezuelan army in the 1980s. The Swedish government confirmed that the weapons had been exported to Venezuela over 20 years earlier, and demanded an explanation. 'We are not going to accept this irresponsibility', Chávez told a televised cabinet meeting. 'We will freeze relations with Colombia.'[28]

Yet another source of inter-American friction is the US' large and relatively unregulated firearms market, which facilitates Latin American organised criminals, since weapons are illegal in their own countries. According to the US State Department's International Narcotics Control Strategy Report for 2009, an estimated 95% of drug-related killings in Mexico were carried out with firearms either purchased or stolen in the US (guns are illegal in Mexico).[29] Around 6,700 gun shops can be found along the US–Mexico border alone. The region has an estimated 16,000 US border patrol agents, but there are only 100 US firearms agents and 35 gun inspectors.[30] In another case, Paraguayan officials have been accused of being involved in the illegal transfer of weapons imports from the US into Brazil.[31]

Illegal arms sales within Latin America are also a problem. Argentina sold arms to Ecuador during the 1995 war with Peru, despite an arms embargo. The Peruvian government has accused members of its security forces of selling Russian anti-aircraft missiles to FARC, an allegation which the Colombian government denies.[32]

Cross-border flows of people contribute to inter-state tension as well. The common belief about migrants in receiving countries is that they take jobs away from willing locals, use publicly funded social services without contributing to the tax base, and are overrepresented in crime statistics. In addition, though not usually considered in discussions of migration, the resentment regarding Brazilians in Paraguay indicates that competition for any scarce factor (land rather than jobs in this case) can create tensions. Because many countries are both sending and receiving countries, the expression of these beliefs can be inconsistent and self-serving, especially since remittances from migrants can also be a major source of income and investment for communities back home.

Migrations have long produced violent confrontations among Latin Americans. In 1937, between 12,000 and 20,000 Haitian migrants were massacred by Dominican police forces during a campaign to expel illegal immigrants. Dominicans today continue to resent and exploit Haitian migrants, and 6,000 were forcibly returned to Haiti in early 2008.[33] Dominicans did provide emergency aid to Haiti after the earthquake in 2010, but one could see this in part as a means of reducing refugee flows into the Dominican Republic. The 1969 war between Honduras and El Salvador, in which up to 4,000 people died, was precipitated by Honduran efforts to expel Salvadoran migrants.

For decades, the Venezuela–Colombia relationship has also been negatively affected by the large number of Colombian migrants into Venezuela.[34] Nicaragua–Costa Rica tensions are influenced by mutual resentment over the presence and treatment of an estimated 400,000 illegal Nicaraguan migrants. Central Americans in Mexico fleeing first the civil war in the 1980s and now economic misery, create issues around labour exploitation (with 45,000 legal workers and 200,000 illegal migrants yearly in Chiapas state alone). Migrants are also victims of criminal gangs and human-rights abuses by authorities on both sides of the border, whether, for example, they are staying in southern Mexico or passing through to the US. Although Guatemala has been understanding of the Mexican situation, in the wake of the unprecedented levels of drug-cartel violence, the pressure by the US and by Mexican citizens for enhanced security on the Guatemalan border will surely increase tensions between the two. Of the 200,000 illegal migrants deported by Mexico in 2006, 47% were Guatemalan, 33% Honduran and 14% Salvadoran.[35] The Chileans have responded positively to Peruvian migrations, adopting a policy that will give amnesty to some 30,000 Peruvians working in the country without documents, an action to which Peruvian President García responded with a declaration of thanks.[36] Relations between Bolivia and Argentina may also be subject to tensions arising from undocumented human flows. Almost half a million Bolivians cross into Argentina to work throughout the economy.[37] Thus multiple relationships across Latin America hold the potential to spark tensions in a context exacerbated by other factors.

The payment of remittances from migrants to their home communities is another area with the potential to affect inter-state relations. Dependence on remittances can add to nationalist sentiments for the defence of a country's migrants, contributing to inter-state tensions. While the US is a major source of remittances, many migrants to Latin American countries also send money home: Nicaraguans from Costa Rica, Bolivians and Paraguayans from Argentina, Peruvians from Chile and Haitians from the Dominican Republic. Though a significant source of national and local income (Mexico peaked at US$24 billion in 2007 and in Haiti, Nicaragua, Honduras and El Salvador the figure represents more than 10% of GDP[38]), remittances have declined in the face of the global recession.

Reduction of remittances can increase domestic tensions, however, since it will increase poverty levels.

An important variation of the immigration phenomenon with significant potential to create tensions is the arrival of increased numbers of Islamic migrants in the Triple Frontier (where Paraguay, Argentina and Brazil meet). The authority of all these governments in this region is weak, contributing to a sense in the hemisphere that the region is a haven for transnational criminal activities. In the case of the terrorist bombings against Jewish community buildings in Argentina, the government identified involvement from Iran, with links to the Triple Frontier. This history, combined with increased Islamic migration and the Iranian diplomatic offensive in the region, may significantly increase concerns over Islamic immigration with the implication of increased risk of terrorism.

International terrorism does not at this time represent a major concern for Latin America, despite US concerns. Rumours that al-Qaeda was recruiting among local Central American gangs, the *maras*, have not been substantiated.[39] A US Drug Enforcement Agency (DEA) sting operation netted an alleged Iranian operative, who has been charged with seeking to use Mexican drug cartels to assassinate the Saudi ambassador to the US.[40] The Spanish-language broadcasting company Unavisión published a documentary alleging extensive Iranian terrorist links in Latin America directed towards US targets,[41] but even Ray Walser of the conservative Heritage Foundation has cautioned that we should not make too much out of these allegations.[42] Argentina suffered from anti-Semitic terrorism traced to Islamic radicals in the Triple Frontier region during the 1990s, but failed to implement serious measures to diminish terrorist financing in the region; in 2012, the Financial Action Task Force (FATF) congratulated Argentina for its passage of anti-money laundering laws in December 2011, but the measures were insufficient to remove Argentina from FATF's strategic deficiency list.[43] Other international terrorist activity included collaboration between the Irish Republican Army (IRA) and FARC. In light of the limited and scattered evidence of terrorist activity in the hemisphere, the region sees other matters as more pressing. Latin American countries also insist on distinguishing between internal rebellion and terrorism. This is why most countries in the region have not labelled FARC as a terrorist organisation, despite US and EU designations.

Still, the region is no stranger to international subversion and there have been instances that contributed to regional tensions. Colombia's government has been fighting guerrillas, drug organisations and right-wing paramilitary forces for decades, with the intensity of violence fluctuating over time as different governments tried distinct mixtures of carrots and sticks. The administration of Alvaro Uribe (2002–2010), with the support of the US government, emphasised use of the stick against two guerrilla groups which also participate in the illegal drug trade, FARC and the Ejército de Liberación Nacional (ELN); in his first year in office, Uribe's successor Santos put out peace feelers, but the guerrillas have not yet responded with firm commitments and continue to ambush soldiers.[44] FARC and the ELN often cross the poorly marked and patrolled borders with Ecuador, Venezuela, Brazil, Peru and Panama for rest, recreation, escape from pursuit and occasional assaults.[45] FARC's current position may lead it to make more desperate efforts to survive, including seeking more active external links as they have in the past, for example with the IRA.[46]

Most Latin American governments have been loath to become involved in Colombia's internal conflict, partly out of fear that it might contaminate their own domestic politics as well as from a historical reluctance to permit third-party intervention in domestic affairs. They tend to ignore it and its limited spillover across isolated borders. The governments of Chávez in Venezuela and Ortega in Nicaragua, in contrast, have given significant rhetorical and material aid to the guerrillas. Colombia has protested and the Uribe government even sent agents to Venezuela in 2004 to kidnap a high-ranking FARC official, provoking one of many diplomatic rows with the Chávez government.[47]

In January 2008, Chávez called for FARC to be granted belligerent status by the international community, which would have imbued the leftist guerrillas with legitimacy and recognition under the Geneva Convention (this case is examined in greater detail in Chapter Three). But after *Operation Phoenix* and the subsequent revelations about FARC's links with the Venezuelan government, Chávez seemed to back off from actively supporting FARC, calling the guerrilla war increasingly unproductive and ill-focused, and stating that history has bypassed the group.[48] As relations between the two administrations blew hot and cold, economic relations boomed, with bilateral trade reaching an estimated US$7bn in 2009.[49] That same year, however, Chávez sacrificed those economic ties to his goal of rhetorically isolating Colombia, because of its agreement permitting the US access to seven of its military bases. Though trade is recovering, some Colombian firms have recovered neither market share nor back payments.

In the wake of the Colombian attack on the FARC camp inside Ecuador, the Uribe government defended the troops' decision to attack the camp, played up the high-value target (Raul Reyes) that was eliminated as a result and accused the Correa and Chávez administrations of providing aid to a group widely recognised as terrorists. Colombians were almost unanimous in their support of the attack. Colombian military action was clearly limited, but sent a warning about what might happen in the future if neighbouring countries did not limit the guerrillas' ability to relocate their camps in the face of increasing Colombian pressure. With Colombia and Venezuela at loggerheads, the decision of the Colombian Supreme Court in August 2010 to require congressional approval of the US bases agreement effectively killed the deal, and when newly elected president Santos offered Venezuela a chance to improve relations, Chávez relented. But as long as FARC and the ELN continue to fight the Colombian government and Venezuela fails to actively collaborate in pursuing them on its side, good relations between the two governments will be at risk.

Though the 2008 incursion was the most widely publicised, Ecuadorian governments have long been concerned about the spillover effects of Colombia's drug-eradication programmes (which include aerial spraying along the border and the possibility that the drug trade might shift more into Ecuador as pressures in Colombia intensify) as well as the guerrilla wars. Many isolated Ecuadorian towns on the border enjoy the economic benefits of providing R&R to FARC, but do not want the fighting if the paramilitaries or the Colombian government implement assassination plots or hot-pursuit strategies. In February 2010, Correa denounced FARC violence within Ecuador.

In Peru, remnants of the Sendero Luminoso (Shining Path) guerrilla movement continue to operate. The Sendero rebels survived the attempts of two successive administrations to destroy them: the second administration of Alan García (2006–2011) and the administration of Ollanta Humala failed to stop operations, and rejected calls by one of the movement's fronts for a negotiated settlement.[50] Although one of the two remaining leaders of Sendero was captured in February 2012, another front remains active; the movement's proven ability to quickly evolve into a major threat, together with the rising social discontent in parts of the country, raises concerns about the consequences of government weakness. Unfortunately, García used the Peruvian concern about a return of terrorism against his domestic opponents by invoking the language of 'terrorism' in conjunction with indigenous protests. After 57 days of peaceful protest by Indians in the jungle regions of Amazonas, Cuscol, Loreto, San Martin and Ucavali, the government sent the armed forces to evict protesters. President García accused the Indians of acting like 'terrorists' and spoke of an 'international conspiracy' in which, according to government ministers, Bolivia and Venezuela are involved.[51] In Bolivia, President Morales and Vice President Alvaro García Linera accuse international NGOs of manipulating indigenous people to undermine the government and oppose the use of natural resources to develop the nation.

These incidents illustrate the complex interconnections linking ideology, subversion, oil-and-gas issues, indigenous movements, and the plastic use of the term 'terrorism' in the volatile inter-state relations of Latin America. Each new incident provides fertile ground for the escalation of inter-state conflicts into militarised inter-state disputes.

The domestic drivers of foreign policy

Inter-state disagreements do not necessarily militarise. One of the determinants of militarisation (Chapter Two examines the others in detail) is the willingness of citizens to support the use of military force in relations with neighbours. To understand that willingness, we need to briefly examine the domestic issues driving politics in the region. All Latin American governments are facing challenges that result from a transition from a less inclusive and corporatist society to a more fully empowered society; unfortunately, a relative lack of social cohesion within Latin American society complicates that transition.[52] Citizen demands for protection against internal threats feed the growing authority and power of the state. What results from the combination of these domestic challenges and responses in a number of Latin American countries is increased nationalism, internal polarisation, and a willingness to go beyond the rule of law in order to right what is perceived to be an injustice.

Distribution of economic gains

The global debt crisis and the need to restructure their economies produced the 'Lost Decade' of the 1980s in Latin America, during which development stalled. The region returned to economic growth in the 1990s, with improvement across all sectors of the population, but the unequal distribution of gains associated with the neo-liberal projects of the period meant that higher income sectors did far better out of the boom than lower-income sectors. At the same time, the gains for many who rose from the category of 'extreme poverty' (defined by the UN Millennium Goals Project as living below US$1 a day) produced little in the way of improvements in quality of life, especially in comparison with the large fortunes visible at the upper levels of society.[53] In Haiti in 2008, thousands rioted in the face of foot shortages, burning tires, blocking highways and looting stores. Not even the UN peacekeeping force could help the police re-establish order.[54] Though Haiti's poverty is extreme, a number of governments (for example, Venezuela and Bolivia) were sufficiently concerned about hunger that they adopted or advocated policies to ensure food supplies at home to avoid such a disruption.

To appreciate the magnitude of economic disparity in Latin America, we need only remember that, for generations, the region has had the sharpest inequality in distribution of resources in the world.[55] For example, in the late 1990s, the top 10% of income earners received 47.2% of income in Brazil, while the figure was 47.0% in Chile and 43.1% in Mexico. In Thailand, Indonesia and South Korea the comparable figures were 32.4%, 28.5% and 22.5%, respectively. In the 1990s and 2000s, the unequal distribution of land decreased in some Latin American countries (Argentina, Honduras, Panama and Peru in the 1990s, Venezuela and Colombia in the 2000s) yet rose in Paraguay and Brazil. Latin America had the highest concentration land ownership in the world, until the countries of Eastern Europe took that mantle after the collapse of communism. Even in the countries with lower concentration *among* landowners (Brazil, Mexico and Colombia), vast numbers of peasants remain landless. Financial assets are the most concentrated of any type of wealth.[56]

When growth slowed or reversed (as it did in Argentina in 1998–2001, Brazil in 2001 and Mexico in 2001) those at the bottom of the social scale tended to lose what small advancement they may have achieved. Recent analysis of a large database of surveys of Latin American and Caribbean households carried out in the period 1989–2004 documents the result of the neo-liberal expansion, namely, mild average increases in inequality since the early 1990s. As the World Bank notes:

> Reducing inequality is one of the main development challenges in Latin America. Inequality is pervasive, resilient, and judged to be fundamentally unfair by many ... In other words, Latinos (sic) are right to feel that they are condemned by a playing field that is not level – it is not.[57]

The implications of such disparity are problematic: an economically polarised country is more likely to be socially and politically unstable. Poverty-reduction programmes that distribute benefits according to political affiliation, as in

Venezuela and Nicaragua, demonstrate to those who do not benefit that, even among the poor, the playing field is not level, thereby increasing ideological tensions.

The perception of many at the bottom – that the neo-liberal reforms of the 1980s and 1990s failed them – produced a backlash against what are seen as market 'excesses'. Latin Americans are not against markets per se; rather, it is the sense that powerful actors have rigged markets against the weak that drives the latter to support increased state intervention in the economy. Even in Chávez's Venezuela, citizen support for markets has increased to almost 70%, and 81% believe that private enterprise is 'indispensible' for the country.[58]

Though an overwhelming majority believes in the market, unhappiness with perceived market excesses has produced a resurgence of nationalist sentiment against globalisation. This is seen most clearly in the nationalisation of not only oil-and-gas fields, but of supermarkets, farms, media companies and other formerly private enterprises whose owners are believed to respond to international market incentives rather than the needs of the local poor. Marginalised sectors of the population blame political elites and their foreign allies (pro-globalisation governments, international capital and international financial institutions) for subordinating the national interest to their private gain.

Populists ride this wave of discontent to power, but then find that they must deliver a constant and significant level of benefits to the previously disenfranchised in order to maintain popular support. Current commodity booms permit governments to be highly inefficient in their poverty-reduction policies, but commodity prices will inevitably decline, rendering these policies unsustainable without significant and politically costly reforms. Once leaders encounter the economic limits of such a scale of redistribution, they will likely cast about for easy targets to blame for the failures that will enrage their constituents. In that context, increased class and ethnic conflict raise the risk of civil war in Bolivia and regime breakdown elsewhere (Venezuela, Ecuador, Peru, Honduras, Guatemala and Nicaragua). In addition to internal conflict, inter-state scapegoating has been a common tactic historically. With increased economic interdependence (for example, Argentina–Chile, Uruguay–Argentina, Nicaragua–Costa Rica) and foreign investment by Latin American countries in neighbouring countries (for example, Brazil in Bolivia, Chile in Peru), blaming one's neighbours for domestic problems can become a serious threat to inter-state relations. The appeal may be greater when one's neighbour is on the other side of the ideological divide.

The ethnic/racial divide

Ethnicity and race are socially constructed categories whose meaning varies across societies. In Latin America there is widespread mixing of indigenous and African heritage peoples and, until recently in most of the region, one's ethnic or racial group was largely determined by social status rather than by blood or genetics. Particularly with respect to indigenous peoples, but also affecting Afro-Latins, social movements have begun to change the politics of identity in order to end their social exclusion and racial discrimination.

The rise of ethnic movements demanding that citizenship should recognise group rights and ethnic self-determination is not peculiar to Latin America, overlapping with the UN recognition of the International Decade of the World's Indigenous People (1995–2004). What is novel is that, for the first time since their largely forced subordination to the nation-state over a century ago, indigenous groups are advancing primarily indigenous claims such as self-determination and cultural pluralism, and only secondarily class claims based on shared interests with peasants, labourers and the urban poor.

The particular importance of this issue for the national context stems from the fact that, oftentimes as in Brazil, Peru and Chile, the relatively remote areas in which the indigenous are concentrated are also the repositories of significant resources that the central government deems essential for national development. Thus the conflicts between indigenous claims of group identity and self-determination are brought into conflict with national claims of resource ownership in an area vital for national economic development.

Increasing state power

The rising power of the state within some countries in the region creates deep mutual distrust both between sectors of society and with other countries. By reinforcing the political–ideological divide, this distrust affects regional relations and erodes public confidence in the government, since it becomes more difficult to develop stable and effective public policies to address the challenges to development that initially gave rise to the ideological divide.

Across Latin America, state power is increasingly manifested in public policy, with nationalisation of private property, distribution of land and price controls on basic foodstuffs, or legislation that opens up environmental and cultural treasures to private exploitation. The opposition (whether it is private media and grocery stores in Venezuela, multinational oil companies in Ecuador or environmental activists and indigenous in Colombia and Peru) becomes polarised when governments of the left and right use the power of the state to stifle opposition.

Of particular concern is the combination of ever-more personalised leadership with greater authority and less accountability that undermines existing constitutions and sometimes produces new constitutions that enhance the power of the president. Though a host of Latin American countries have enacted constitutional reforms allowing at least one re-election of the president, this is only a concern for our purposes when the constitutional reform was likely to have been obtained through non-democratic means. For example, in a second attempt at constitutional reform in Venezuela in 2009, Chávez was able to gain majority support for unlimited re-election for all public officials, though charges have been levelled concerning coercion of public employees and the poor in order to attain this result.[59]

In Nicaragua, Daniel Ortega seems to be pursuing a combination of fraudulent elections, corrupt manipulation of the courts and orchestrated violence to secure his role.[60] It would be a mistake, though, to see Nicaragua as simply another 'Boliviarian' state. Ortega is neither a 'chavista' nor a link to the Sandinista past. Indeed, the Frente Sandinista de Liberación Nacional (FSLN) split with him over his personalist agenda, and he is even allied with forces on the right. For example, his vice-president, Jaime Morales Carazo, is a former member of the Contra rebels that fought the Sandinista government in the 1980s with US support. Ortega also supported the ban on therapeutic abortions in return for support from the Catholic Church.

One reason why many Latin American leaders have succeeded in gaining more authority is because personal insecurity is a fundamental challenge for many Latin Americans.[61] Particularly in democratising countries, the decline in personal security, and use of the military for domestic crime fighting (all but two countries, Chile and Argentina, have used the military to supplement the police[62]) have had variable but potentially profound political implications. In virtually all of Latin America, deficiencies in police forces, judicial systems and investigations make it easier for crime to flourish and for an overzealous criminal justice system to infringe on citizen rights.[63]

According to opinion polls from Latinobarómetro, the region historically shifts between identifying economic problems as the most important issue, and choosing crime instead. Even with the serious global economic recession, however, in 2009 seven Latin American countries still listed crime as the number-one problem facing the country. Venezuela and Panama topped the list, with 55% and 45%, respectively, naming crime as the most important problem. The other countries where crime was ranked first (by between 24% and 32% of respondents) were Costa Rica, El Salvador, Uruguay, Chile and Guatemala. On average in 2009, Latin American countries named crime as the second most important problem.[64]

Violent crime has received the most attention, whether it is perpetrated by *maras* or by drug trafficking organisations (DTOs). In fact, the Caribbean and Central and South America are among the most violent regions in the world.[65] Even countries in which perceptions of crime were relatively benign, such as Panama, have seen a significant increase in violent crime associated with gangs, guerrillas and drugs.[66]

As concerns about crime and violence have risen, proposals proliferate to decrease crime by increasing the capacity of the police, often buttressed by the military.[67] Unfortunately, the increase in equipment, expectations, and political leeway accorded the police and the military in domestic operations across the region have resulted in significant human-rights abuses. In Chile, the president from the right, Sebastián Piñero, made being tough on crime the centrepiece of his successful campaign to unseat the centre-left coalition after 20 years in power and despite the high popularity of the outgoing President Michelle Bachelet.

Government-perpetrated violence in the name of fighting crime is becoming a major threat to citizen security in some countries. In Paraguay, police harassed, tortured and threatened to burn alive landless peasants who were demanding land reform.[68] In Colombia, governments have consistently been accused of either using right-wing paramilitaries directly to kill or intimidate opposition, or of tolerating these activities in order to reap the benefits of a coerced opposition indirectly. Uribe's 'democratic security' campaign in Colombia provided the military with some police powers, increased the size of the police force by 10,000 and also created a network of 100,000 paid informants; the programme includes few safeguards on the abuse of power by the authorities.[69] A strong far-right sentiment and some spectacular successes in killing or capturing FARC leaders bolstered Uribe's position, but the guerrillas have not been defeated, nor have they decided to negotiate a surrender, thus remaining a threat to Colombia. Upon taking office, President Santos extended an invitation to the guerrillas to negotiate peace if they would cease their fighting. It is not clear, were it to agree to take part in talks, whether FARC would negotiate in good faith. In the late 1990s it used peace negotiations as a respite to fortify itself and return to its operations. In challenges at the opposite end of the political spectrum, the Santos government has not been able to protect either labour leaders or journalists from right-wing extremists, as evidenced by the fact that in the first five months of 2011 'more than a dozen journalists have been declared "military targets" by paramilitary groups, and, on May 26, guerrilla forces are suspected of trying to kill an investigative reporter'.[70]

Conclusion

Even as many Latin American citizens are demanding that their governments respond more assertively to threats at home and from fellow citizens, we should not be surprised when citizens support their governments in taking a forceful stand against a neighbouring state believed to be either encroaching on or threatening national interests. The fact that many inter-state issues have been resolved peacefully does not increase the likelihood that future issues can be defused without resorting to violence. As we have seen, there are many problems that remain potential flashpoints, capable of eliciting strong responses, including militarisation.

CHAPTER TWO

The dynamics of militarisation

The decision to use military force to address an inter-state dispute is made at the higher levels of civilian government and the armed forces. Using military force to defend one's interests is most usefully conceived of as a rational decision, taken under consideration of certain goals and information about opportunities and constraints. Therefore, we need to consider those goals and the information available to policymakers in order to understand when they may choose to militarise their disagreements.

The long-standing pattern in Latin America is for leaders to avoid major war, while still using military force to influence their relations with other states in the region. Military force is still seen as a legitimate tool in relations with neighbouring Latin American states. The key questions for leaders considering militarising a dispute are whether the use of military force will benefit their constituencies at a cost that they are willing to pay, and whether the leaders can survive their displeasure if the costs are high. While leaders do not calculate infallibly, they do make decisions with the expectation that the benefits of their decision will outweigh the costs.

As discussed earlier, there are many sources of inter-state tensions and the domestic context for addressing them is becoming more unstable in many countries. Though not every country in the region is encountering serious difficulties in addressing these challenges, those that are not (Uruguay and Chile stand out) cannot isolate themselves from the negative fallout, should their neighbours be undermined by these challenges.

Violence as a means to resolve internal conflict is gaining acceptance across the region once again and nationalist rhetoric is raising the perceived value of many topics in dispute among neighbouring states, making it increasingly likely that the costs of using force to achieve nationalist goals are becoming acceptable. Arms purchases and diplomatic activism have made the strategic balance in the region ambiguous, making it possible for countries seeking change ('revisionist states') to think that perhaps their own military weakness can be offset by the 'justice' of their case and the resources of friendly countries. Some leaders (for example, Morales and Santos) may find themselves encouraged by certain constituencies to pursue those nationalist goals using the nation's armed forces. Other leaders, such as Chávez and Ortega, face diminishing constraints on the decision to militarise as their accountability to their constituencies decreases. This trend makes it more likely that a leader may take the risk of militarisation to pursue his personal agenda for the international dispute, since constituents are unlikely to be able to punish any misjudgement of the costs of such an action.

Understanding militarisation
The use of military force is not an irrational decision, however poor the consequences of that use may turn out to be. In the aftermath of the disastrous and bloody Chaco War between

Bolivia and Paraguay in the mid-1930s (in which up to 100,000 people perished), Latin American leaders have sought to avoid major war while nevertheless using low levels of military force to alter the bargaining context with their rivals.[1] In the evaluation of constituency costs, leaders understand that constituents are willing to pay higher costs if they greatly value the goal; rising nationalism has the effect of increasing the value of issues in dispute with other countries. A constituency's ability to influence the leader depends on the institutional structure of accountability, which is highest in consolidated liberal democracies and decreases as leaders become more empowered to use state authority to deal with perceived threats to national interests, whether at the domestic or international level. The balance among costs, constituents' willingness to pay, and constituents' ability to influence the leader forms the basis of the decision regarding militarisation.

The Argentine miscalculations that led to the Falklands/Malvinas War in 1982 demonstrate that leaders and citizens are not infallible in making these calculations, because the relevant information may be missing, incomplete or ambiguous. In the Falklands/Malvinas case, citizens celebrated wildly when the Argentine military seized the islands, because they were not expecting the British to respond militarily, nor to win if they did. Once the costs of the war rose, the Argentines began regretting having militarised the dispute, and defeat unleashed their fury against a military government whose earlier sins (in a brutal dictatorship) had been significantly forgotten in the euphoria surrounding the seizure of the islands.

The model we propose for understanding the decision to militarise indicates that a leader may choose to use force only when the costs produced by the combination of political–military strategy chosen, the strategic balance and the characteristics of the force used are equal to or lower than the costs acceptable to the leader's constituency, though this last factor may also be affected by the slippage in accountability produced by the domestic means of selecting leaders. Accountability means that the leader must respond to demands of the constituency; therefore, should the constituency demand forceful action, this variable will push for militarisation. Force will not always be used when these conditions are met, but the likelihood of its use will increase and force will not be used in their absence.

After a decade in which the variables determining the use of force all moved against its deployment, in a number of countries some of these variables have begun shifting back towards encouraging militarisation. The fact that these key variables are under stress reveals the potential for militarised conflict to proliferate, even developing into more severe threats to security in the region.

Political–military strategies

Advancing national interests by militarising a dispute can be pursued through different political–military strategies, depending upon the relationship between the contending parties. These alternatives can be usefully summarised in the following seven possible political–military strategies:

- achieving a military conquest;
- diverting attention from domestic problems;
- keeping the issue in dispute alive;
- affecting bilateral negotiations;
- defending the status quo;
- attracting the support of third parties; and
- imposing a solution.

The political–military strategies for using force have not changed. Latin Americans still do not seek military conquest of their rivals, even when they claim significant portions of their territory, as in the case of Venezuela's claim of two-thirds of Guyana. Sometimes militarising a dispute at a particular moment can serve as a diversionary manoeuvre by a government which is under domestic stress. But, in such circumstances, governments may only hope to militarise a dispute as a diversion if there were an issue that had already risen to the level of inter-state tensions (for example, Bolivia's frustration with Chile's continued refusal to consider sovereign access to the sea; Argentina's concern that oil and gas exploration around the Malvinas/Falklands would yield large discoveries and thus make the UK even less willing to negotiate sovereignty), otherwise a decision to militarise the issue would be too transparent to generate more than a short-term surge of nationalist support for the government. Thus diversion is rarely a strategy chosen on its own merits, but is most likely to be chosen when inter-state tensions are already high: rarely does it constitute the *reason* for tensions being high. Weak, revisionist states continue to want to keep the issues they dispute with more powerful neighbours alive, but unlike the Ecuador–Peru dispute that led to the war in 1995, in only one current case in Latin America is a party to a dispute unwilling to recognise that an issue exists; consequently, there is no need in the vast majority of disputes to resort to a political–military strategy to keep the issue alive. For example, Bolivia continues to demand a sovereign access to the sea through Chile, but until now the Chileans have undercut the attraction for a Bolivian leader to militarise by demonstrating that Chile is willing to discuss possible solutions without explicitly ruling out sovereign access. The Bolivians have been able to articulate their demands in international forums, such as the OAS, the UN and the Vatican, so the issue retains a high profile. The one exception is Argentina's claim to the Malvinas/Falkland Islands: the UK refuses to acknowledge a need for sovereignty negotiations. The Argentines see the issue as simply a question of how to transfer sovereignty, since they see UK control as an anachronistic remnant of the colonial era. Argentina, however, has been able to keep the issue alive at the OAS and the UN, and all Argentine governments since the 1982 war have understood that the country has no domestic or international support for militarising its demands for the British to negotiate.

Because a number of issues are being discussed between rival nations, the potential to use militarisation as a means to affect bilateral talks or the current tenor of relations arises. When the Chávez government in Venezuela was engaged in acrimonious phases of its relationship with the Colombian government of Uribe, for example, Chávez used militarily belligerent rhetoric aimed at persuading the Colombian people and government that taking a tough stance with Venezuela would be costly. This tactic, used frequently but often unsuccessfully in international relations (for example, US and Israeli military responses to terrorism which result in increased popular support for the terrorists), failed to achieve Chavez's goal. Colombia under Uribe persisted in its anti-Chávez posture. Chávez has responded to the conciliatory overtures of Uribe's successor, Juan Manuel Santos, by refraining from threatening rhetoric and offering conciliatory gestures even at some domestic costs to himself, as seen in the arrest and extradition to Colombia of a suspected FARC fundraiser in April 2011.[2] This change in tone suggests that Chávez is aware that Santos will enjoy an initial period of support at home, during which he may judge whether his conciliatory policies deliver more security than Uribe's confrontations with Chávez. Thus, Chávez would have little ability to pressure Santos for greater concessions regarding the guerrillas and regional relations. Consequently, the effort to affect domestic politics within Colombia in order to pressure Santos has been put on the back burner.

Of course, states content with the current situation (status-quo states) may consider using threats to dissuade the revisionists. British declarations of willingness and ability to militarily defend the Falklands against Argentine claims of sovereignty come to mind. The next step up, actual displays of force, are also quite commonly used to affect relations. These include Colombian military displays on San Andres Island directed against Nicaragua in 2007 and 2008; and Brazilian military manoeuvres and rhetoric during the Brazilian and Paraguayan governments' discussions in 2008 of difficult bilateral issues relating to energy and the rights of Brazilian farmers in Paraguay.

Militarisation of a dispute can also be a means of attempting to attract third-party support for one's position by provoking a crisis. Ecuador successfully utilised this tactic in 1995 against Peru, achieving a settlement in 1998 that it would not have received had not the four guarantor countries (Argentina, Brazil, Chile and the United States) of the 1941 peace treaty between the Ecuador and Peru played active roles out of fear the dispute could escalate into a full-scale war. The regional security architecture's weak constraints on 'moral hazard' encourage this type of response (for more details, see Chapter Four). Bolivian frustration with Chile has been growing, presenting the potential temptation to create an incident that would stimulate third parties to step in to demand concessions from the Chileans in the name of hemispheric peace.

The last Latin American example of a political–military strategy to impose a solution to a dispute is the Argentine seizure of the Malvinas/Falklands Islands in 1982. Nicaragua, however, has come close. The militarisation of the San Juan River dispute in 1998 by Nicaragua signalled the seriousness with which it interpreted the clause in its boundary treaty with Costa Rica which required that country to request permission for its armed personnel to transit the river. Since the case went to the ICJ for resolution (2005–2008), it may be argued that militarisation was not designed to impose a solution in this matter, but to raise the profile of the issue to force progress towards resolution. But the decision to use troops in 2010 to protect dredging operations in territory that had been widely recognised as Costa Rican (and thereby recreate a reference point that was cited in an 1898 surveyor's report regarding the border) was an effort to impose a solution. Costa Rica filed a case at the ICJ in 2011, but by the time the court ordered the parties to desist from further action until it could rule on the case, the Nicaraguans had completed their dredging operations. Though imposition of a solution generally requires larger-scale military force than that used by Nicaragua in 2010, the fact that Costa Rica does not have a military permitted the low-level use of force to be effective.

Strategic balance

The concept of strategic balance helps us understand the bargaining situation between countries, and is a second factor to consider in evaluating the potential costs of militarising a dispute. Strategic balance is a relative measure, referring to the factors which influence the likely costs produced by the strategies each actor can use in particular disputes, rather than in its more narrow military sense. Thus we need to consider what kinds of diplomatic, economic and military responses to militarisation can be anticipated, and what costs they will likely generate. Because of incomplete and private information, the strategic balance is never entirely clear to either party. As we shall see in Chapter Three, however, the strategic balance has become increasingly ambiguous in the pairs of states, or dyads, where disputes continue, despite the declarations in favour of peaceful resolution of conflict by regional organisations.

The diplomatic resources relevant to evaluation of the costs of militarisation revolve around the ability to garner external support for, and blunt external criticism of, one's strategy in the dispute. The parties to a militarised dispute welcome mediation when neither believes it has the military capacity to impose a solution unilaterally. The diplomatic balance is affected not just by the skill of the diplomatic corps, but also by the standing which one's position on the disputed issue has in the international arena. For example, the US would certainly condemn and sanction the use of military force by Chávez's Venezuela against Colombia. But in the 2008 Colombian incursion into Ecuador, Colombia's major ally, the US, was supportive of Colombian efforts to eliminate such a high-value target, even if in doing so it violated the sovereignty of a country that did not appear much interested in dealing with the problem. This situation largely parallels the US raid on Osama bin Laden's compound in Pakistan in 2011. Colombia also had to know that other Latin American states would denounce its use of force against FARC in Ecuador, but it did not expect any long-term fallout from its decision.

The diplomatic costs that would accompany a militarisation have always been low because of regional reluctance to assign blame, and in some key dyads these costs are declining. The willingness of regional organisations to pay the political costs of confronting a recalcitrant state in a militarised conflict has historically been limited for two reasons: the organisations prefer to have both parties request help, and it takes time for the organisation to meet and decide on a course of action. In the 1995 war, Ecuador and Peru declared and violated multiple ceasefires over 34 days before an arrangement could be worked out for the four guarantors to dispatch forces to ensure a separation of the two armies.[3] The slow multilateral response means that a government engaged in provocative behaviour can expect to make at least short-term gains before having to respond to regional pressures for peaceful resolution. Although the March 2008 Colombian incursion into Ecuador generated Latin American diplomacy that defused the crisis, it still took four days to get the process under way, and Colombia never came to perceive that the costs of that attack on Ecuadorian soil outweighed its benefits. The wars between Argentina and the UK (1982) and Ecuador and Peru (1995) demonstrated that a weaker state could hold out for weeks against a more powerful state unable to mobilise its military resources quickly. Argentina did not benefit from this lag-time, whereas Ecuador was able to secure a settlement that had eluded it for 50 years. But if the weak state cannot hold out, the diplomatic protection the regional security architecture offers might not be mobilised in time, resulting in an embarrassing military defeat, as when Peru responded successfully to Ecuadorean incursions into disputed territory in 1981.

In contrast to regional norms, there are efforts, spearheaded by Hugo Chávez, to create an alternative diplomatic venue that would countenance the use of force as a self-proclaimed defensive measure and judge which states are aggressors. Chávez seeks to create a bloc of nations in the hemisphere that excludes the US and Canada, and which would be pro-Bolivarian and anti-US. The expectation is that it would be quick to condemn actions against states supportive of the Bolivarian agenda set by Chávez and supportive of any militarisations in defence of Bolivarian governments. That includes not just the oft-proclaimed war that would ensue if Venezuela were invaded by the US, but also the dispatch of Venezuelan military aid to any ally that might request it – as Chávez offered in 2008 when the Morales government faced potential insurrection in eastern Bolivia.[4]

These efforts have so far produced a bloc of states under the Alianza Bolivariana para los pueblo de nuestra America

(ALBA, the Bolivarian Alliance of the Peoples of our America), but Chávez's support for UNASUR and the Organisation of Latin American and Caribbean Nations also fits into this strategy. Some of these nations (Bolivia and Venezuela) may already be facing sanctions by the US and thus they will be unlikely to see additional costs coming from that side; but they will be attracted by the prospect of support from the new regional organisations. Already, the newcomers to the regional security scene have been making their presence felt. ALBA issued a joint statement in early 2011 demanding that the OAS stay out of Venezuelan affairs; this was in response to a petition sent to the OAS by Venezuelan students, who wanted the organisation to investigate claims of political prisoners in Venezuela.[5] This sign of Chávez's assertiveness on the regional stage raises questions about the diplomatic balance: because he is willing to assign blame, the question of whether he would follow through with sanctions and military aid and whether the new organisations would follow his lead becomes relevant. Whether militarisation would occur, depends not only on this variable of the diplomatic balance, but on how the other variables play out in the particular case.

The influence of a second component of the strategic balance, economic resources, is twofold. Economic resources include both those that can be used in a non-military way to influence behaviour by a rival, and those for building up national capacity to use military force. In evaluating whether to use military force, policymakers will consider both aspects of economic power. When economic leverage over a rival is sufficient to gain one's goals at acceptable costs, force is unlikely to be used.[6] Venezuela seems to have chosen to use economic inducements rather than force in its relations with Guyana (it claims two-thirds of Guyanan territory). Chief among these is its proposal to supply subsidised oil through the PetroCaribe programme, under which it already sends subsidised crude oil to Caribbean states since 2005.[7] This is in marked contrast to a militarised incident in 2007, during which Guyana claimed its larger neighbour had sent troops to destroy dredges and had flown unauthorised aircraft sorties in Guyanan airspace.[8] But when economic leverage is deemed insufficient, how economic resources affect a state's ability to mobilise, use and resupply military forces becomes paramount.

Within the context of inter-state rivalry, leaders will also evaluate the appropriateness of their military resources in the event that economic and diplomatic means are insufficient to influence a rival's behaviour. The decision to augment them in the appropriate categories to best position themselves to militarise the issue brings to the fore the ability to raise revenue for defence by highlighting the domestic opportunity costs. The greater the opportunity costs, the more likely that opposition to its use will form. For example, the inability of a state to tax the wealthy in a poor country imposes a severe constraint on state expenditures, and that is a general problem for most Latin American countries.[9] Military expenditures thus come more openly at the expense of expenditures on economic and social welfare. In the 1980s and 1990s military budgets were cut because of the economic crises most Latin American nations faced just at the time that democracy was returning to the region. But high commodity prices can offset that weak domestic taxing power, and Latin American governments have benefitted from this factor since 2003.[10] Paying for the ability to display or use low levels of force certainly does not seem to be contested by domestic constituents today, however. Even Costa Rica, which does not have an army, has created a new border unit in its National Police force to challenge Nicaraguan encroachment.[11]

Military resources, the third factor to consider in evaluating the strategic balance, includes the quality and quantity of personnel, type and quantity of armaments, and doctrines for utilising those resources and alliances. Studies of great-power foreign policy tend to emphasise the quantitative aspect of such resources, because the social and economic disparities that underlie qualitative differences among great powers are not large. But the experiences of Israel in the Middle East and Chile in South America demonstrate the importance of quality differentials where they exist.

The quantity and quality of military personnel matters in rivalries. The Chileans have historically been outmanned and outgunned in their traditional conflict hypothesis of being surrounded by three threats: Peru, Bolivia and Argentina. But the Chileans' reputation for military skill enabled them to come out of the 1976–78 war crises with all three countries without firing a shot or backing down.[12] That difference continues today: Peruvian pilots, for example, do not receive sufficient flying time or instruction to be on a par with their Chilean counterparts.[13]

There is some concern that a significant expansion of the armed forces via the creation of citizen militias can be destabilising to regional rivalries. According to Chávez, the militias have two missions: to protect the beneficiaries of land reform from landowner-financed mercenaries and to defend the Bolivarian Revolution from foreign intervention.[14] Domestically, the development of a civilian militia in Venezuela is a potential threat for its democracy, because the opposition fears that it will be used against legitimate dissension. The militias are less likely to be a regionally destabilising factor. Colombian armed forces are unlikely to consider Venezuelan militia to be a deterrent in a conflict scenario, because the former would probably remain very close to the border if they cross it, while the latter are far from the border. Only a country seeking to occupy Venezuela and change its government would need to consider the presence and effectiveness of militia; since no Latin American country contemplates such a mission, the only potential external enemy for which Venezuela's militia would be relevant would be the US.

Armed personnel performing regular duties along border areas lower potential costs of militarising a dispute, since their presence is already paid for and accepted by citizens for reasons that may have little to do with inter-state rivalry. Stationing troops along borders to combat transnational crime requires coordination to avoid accidental confrontations by armed personnel of the two bordering nations. Colombia and Brazil, which have no major issues in dispute, understand this potential and are developing the necessary communication channels; Venezuela and Colombia have also discussed setting up a bilateral committee to oversee border relations.[15] Yet Bolivia and Chile or Nicaragua and Costa Rica, both with contentious issues between them, have each taken independent measures in pursuing transnational crime and thus their actions provoke concern for each rival.

According to the IISS *Military Balance* volumes, the type and quantity of Latin American military capabilities are developing. SIPRI reports that South American military expenditures experienced the highest increase in the world in 2011,[16] and that 'transfers to South America were 150% higher during the last five years compared to the beginning of the millennium, following a significant upswing in both military spending and orders for arms in recent years.'[17] Following the significant cuts in prior decades, recent significant rises still put Latin American militaries on a relatively modest military footing, with the possible exception of Brazil. Many Latin Americans do not care how their militaries stand up to others in an international context, since they do not anticipate extra-regional use. They do worry, however, that expansion of military capabilities increases potential damage in the event that fighting breaks out between Latin American nations. Concerns from both analysts and governments regarding potential arms races in the region reflect not only the significant increase in armaments, but also the lack of trust and transparency in the regional context within which these purchases are being carried out.

The Washington Office on Latin America (WOLA) notes that arms purchases in the region are characterised by a lack of transparency and poor diplomatic communication,[18] which makes it difficult not only to know who is purchasing what, but also how the military balance is being affected. Though there have been efforts to increase transparency in the defence sector in the past, and UNASUR has taken up the baton currently, past efforts have failed, generating little confidence that UNASUR will succeed. In the context of a regional rivalry in which Peruvians have always considered the Chileans as aggressive, the increased number of combat aircraft and superior technology of the submarine fleet is alarming. According to *Jane's Defense Weekly*, Chile replaced its 12 ageing *Mirage* aircraft with 18 F-16s; and it also has a superior submarine fleet.[19] Venezuela's military modernisation project cost well over US$4 billion and included combat aircraft, tanks, attack helicopters, coastal patrol boats and 100,000 assault rifles. Possible future purchases include more tanks, aircraft, naval vessels, surface-to-air missiles and air-defence systems.[20] The Russian jets, particularly with unseasoned Venezuelan pilots, are no match for US fighter jets. Though a Colombian security analyst suggested that Russian pilots could fly them in a conflict with Colombia, it is highly unlikely that the Russian government would be willing to risk open military confrontation with the US and general condemnation in the Western Hemisphere in order to aid Chávez. So against whom might Venezuela's offensive capabilities be utilised? Several candidates merit consideration. Venezuela disputes territory with Guyana and Colombia (one of the justifications for Chávez's failed 1992 coup was the government's inability to defend those claims) in addition to long-running tensions about FARC.[21] Another possible candidate is Chile, with could draw Venezuela into a conflict concerning Bolivia's access to the sea.[22]

Extra-regional arms manufacturers may be increasing their stimuli to greater arms purchases in the region. For example, licensing French armaments through Brazilian factories or Russian through Venezuelan ones could increase the pace of modernisation and create economic and employment arguments for continuing to sell arms within the region, once the 'modernisation to fill the gap from the 1980s' argument is no longer relevant. There is also widespread concern that Venezuelan-manufactured arms, particularly Kalashnikov rifles, could be made available to insurgent groups who identify with Chávez's Bolivarian goals and seek to overthrow their governments.

Arms purchases in Latin America are not for the sake of a prestige-oriented modernisation. Given the history of US invasions in the region, as well as that country's contemporary behaviour elsewhere, Venezuela has legitimate fears about a US-led invasion. Chile is apprehensive about militarised incidents generating pressure by third parties for concessions to Bolivia, and so continues to think about the need to very quickly gain control over any militarised incident. Colombia's civil war has dragged on for decades, even before Venezuela and Ecuador began providing at least tacit support for the guerrillas, so the Colombian government has a legitimate interest in increasing its military capabilities. Brazil has for some time been developing its ability to protect its rights to exploit the Amazon in line with national development plans, despite international concerns about the environment. Now that it has discovered vast hydrocarbon reserves in its exclusive economic zone, it is concerned about protecting those deposits from seizure by a potential foe as well.

Though not as significant for militarisation short of war, this dramatic growth in armaments would be a major factor, were escalation to move towards war. Despite the fact that few want war when militarisation is initiated, the 1982 and 1995 wars in the region demonstrate that escalation can occur, and thus the overall military balance carries weight in decisions about militarisation.

The modernisation of military structures, with civilian-led ministries and Joint General Staffs in many countries, is part of a major change in military doctrine that began with the return of democracy in the 1980s, with Latin American governments emphasising civilian control. The US Departments of State and Defense in their relationships with Latin America promote not only civilian control, but orientations towards fighting crime and international peacekeeping. Many US and Latin American advocates of civilian control believe that providing Latin American militaries with peacekeeping experiences in Haiti or around the globe will keep them out of domestic politics, build confidence among Latin American militaries, and decrease their focus on regional rivalries.

Despite the positive potential, we should be cautious of the impact of peacekeeping. Historically, Latin American militaries have overthrown governments that were perceived to be incapable of providing domestic order, often with significant popular support. In addition, inter-state tensions have developed when a country has perceived that domestic instability is being fed by a neighbour. In this context, the international peacekeeping experience of Latin American officers may heighten concerns when they return home as officers observe their own government's weakness in dealing with social unrest;

it may also increase regional tensions to the degree that neigh-bours are perceived as stoking internal instability. For example, Brazilian intelligence and military were concerned about Paraguayan contacts with the landless-peasant movement in Brazil that has seen violent confrontations; the Honduran military and opposition that overthrew President Zelaya accused Chávez of fomenting Honduran instability; and Peru has accused Bolivia of stimulating indigenous confrontations. Brazil, Honduras and Peru have all participated in peacekeep-ing operations abroad. Though this question has not yet been rigorously explored, the studies of domestic instability and military coups in the 1960s by Alfred Stepan and Luigi Einaudi provide a basis for concern.[23]

Latin American militaries continue to see national defence in a regional context as their major mission. The evolution of military doctrines in their view is intended to increase capabil-ities through improved efficiency, unified strategic planning, joint training and doctrinal development, and appropriate arms procurement. Few Latin American countries, however, can effectively implement these changes in practice; those that can (Brazil and Chile stand out) will improve their relative positions in Latin America's military arena.

Military doctrines in the Bolivarian group of nations have also begun to put greater emphasis upon 'asymmetric warfare' than in the past and the contribution of citizen militias to defence, although conventional, tactical deterrence still plays a large part in procurements. Among this group, only Venezuela has articulated a view of a neighbour (Colombia) as a strategic enemy, though not coherently nor consistently by any means. As we have seen, in the early days of the Santos administration, Chávez focused on a cooperative relationship, but that could alter quickly and dramatically if Chávez changes his mind or he is replaced by one of the more radical members of his group as a result of his illness. Though for reasons already articulated, the Venezuelan militia are unlikely to confront the Colombian military, Venezuela perceives itself as better prepared to confront an enemy, having adopted asymmetric strategy into its doctrine and planning. In addition, recent adjustments in Venezuela's Organic Law of the National Armed Force permit the president to send the armed forces into a hostile country to pre-empt an attack against Venezuela.[24] Thus Venezuela's doctrinal evolution could be particularly destabilising for the region.

New alliances have been developing and they may have an impact on the perception of the military balance between rivals. One especially key alliance revolves around the Chávez regime in Venezuela, which is a beacon to close allies at the head of the weak revisionist states of Bolivia, Ecuador and Nicaragua. Though these latter governments may now perceive that the regional context has moved in their favour, the 'beacon' is, in reality, not as strong a signal as Chávez might have us believe. The uncertainty created by the 'Chávez Axis' arises because the Venezuelan leader puts out a great deal of rhetoric about his willingness to come to the military aid of his allies should they be attacked, but his actions are non-transparent, leaving rivals no clear basis for assessing actual risk. For example, Venezuela provides military assistance to Bolivia, but without revealing how much or what types. This lack of transparency is particularly difficult to read because Chávez's credibility is questionable: despite his belligerent tone in the Colombia–Ecuador crisis and his offer to send troops to defend the Morales government when a coup plot was discovered, no one knows how far Chávez will go in economic and military terms to support his allies. His sudden call in June 2008 for FARC to release all of its 700+ hostages and negotiate a peaceful settlement was completely unanticipated and befuddling to observers.[25] And of course his battle with cancer in 2011 and the fact that he has no designated successor, should he be unable to govern through illness or death, further contribute to the instability of this alliance. No one knows if Chávez will be emboldened to push faster to achieve his regional goals or whether he will be distracted and discouraged about his future role in the hemisphere. The former would certainly be destabilising, while the latter would contribute to regional stability.

Another potential factor to consider in discussion of Latin American militaries is Russia. Stephen Blank believes that Russia wants to use its ability to supply weapons and intelligence to Venezuela and Ecuador to facilitate their support of FARC, though after the 2008 incident with Colombia the Correa government appears to have re-evaluated its relations with FARC. In this interpretation, the claim is that Russia would benefit from Colombia's need for the US to continue to provide significant support and thus have less ability to counter Russian influence elsewhere.[26] China has sold military goods to Venezuela, Bolivia, Ecuador, Argentina and Brazil (a sale of tanks to Peru was cancelled after the military's budget was cut in 2011) and its loans to Latin American countries also help weaken the budget constraint and thus contribute indirectly to increased military procurement, especially since many of these loans come with few strings attached on their use. In addition, the Chinese have been increasing contacts at the military-to-military level and held their first joint military exercise in 2010 with Peru.[27]

Traditionally, the US could tip the balance on a dispute in the region. But US capabilities and its credibility in the region have deteriorated. The US has no real military influence on local power balances beyond Colombia. Though the 2008 reactivation of the Fourth Fleet based in Florida sparked concern among South American states, particularly since not even pro-US Chile was consulted on the decision, no other South American country would likely facilitate US naval operations against another country on the continent. The development of a closer Colombian–US alliance to fight the FARC/ELN/other drug traffickers worried states throughout the region that the US was pushing the militarised drug trade conflict further into the region as producers and traffickers sought to avoid the US' reach. But the less pro-US policy of President Santos and the increased involvement of the US in fighting the drug cartels in Mexico and Central America seem to have diminished concerns in South America over US intentions in the southern hemisphere.

Characteristics of force

This factor refers to the specific type of force that is to be used in militarising the dispute, and is the third component that illuminates the costs to be expected in militarisation. In this sense, the characteristics of force a government chooses to use reflects military capabilities and the specific context in which militarisation occurs, that is, the fit between the armaments an action utilises and the context it is addressing. The two important factors to consider here are force alternatives and mobilisation requirements. Examples of the former include whether the decision will entail a local platoon setting up at the border in a display of force, an over-flight violating sovereignty but with little chance of a direct confrontation, actual engagement of troops and the mobilisation of a large support group, and a myriad of other combinations across the spectrum of engagement. The key issues around mobilisation are time and the personal and economic costs to society of the disruption. So, for example, use of a reserve-based military would be very disruptive to members of society and to the economy, whereas use of a standing army would carry lower mobilisation costs;

in addition, if the standing army were comprised of conscripts, the mobilisation costs would be felt across society, whereas if it were a volunteer army those costs would be concentrated among the social group that tends to see the military as an economic opportunity.

The characteristics of force that could be used in a conflict in Latin America have changed in tandem with the rebuilding of the military – they are getting more sophisticated and offense-capable, which can lead to perceptions that quick military successes may be more likely now without requiring large mobilisation of human and economic resources. In this increasingly uncertain regional context, military modernisation can fuel uncertainty and suspicion as nations claim their purchases simply offset neighbours' prior purchases. Honduran military aircraft increase tension with Nicaragua, which refuses to destroy more SAM-7 missiles unless Honduras and El Salvador rid themselves of military aircraft.[28] Chile's force modernisation raises concerns in Peru that it has accomplished not only 'modernisation', but also a significant increase in relative power. Venezuela's plans to produce Kalashnikovs, combined with claims that the specific calibre of ammunition used in these Kalashnikovs are also useable in FARC's older models, raises fears about leakage from the Venezuelan Army to guerrilla groups in the region.[29]

The agreement by the Uribe administration to provide the US with access to seven military bases, replacing the one at Manta that Ecuador did not renew, was poised to dramatically decrease the potential costs for Colombia of using its air assets against neighbouring countries. Such usage was not merely theoretical: in March 2008, Colombia did use aircraft to carry out a swift and effective attack against a target across the border in Ecuador. The US would have upgraded the Colombian military installations and would have been in close communication with any Colombian personnel planning and operating cross-border strikes. The base agreement highlighted bilateral cooperation 'in areas such as interoperability, joint procedures, logistics and equipment, training and instruction, intelligence exchanges, surveillance and reconnaissance capabilities, combined exercises and other mutually agreed activities'.[30] The Colombian Supreme Court's requirement that Congress approve the base agreement has postponed concerns over the regional security implications of that agreement for now.

Permanent deployment of military forces in border regions substantially reduces time and incremental costs of mobilisation. To fight crime in the border area with Bolivia, the Chilean government is reinforcing the border with personnel and physical barriers to make illegal crossing more difficult. While they are focused on crime, these actions will make it more difficult for Bolivia to consider provoking an incident to attract third-party attention, since Chilean forces would be likely to quickly control any incident before a third party might decide that it could escalate to war were Chile not pressured to make significant concessions.[31] In an example that demonstrates this point, uniformed but sparsely armed Bolivian soldiers were arrested on 14 June 2011 on the Chilean side of the border; their weapons were seized and they were released after two days.[32] The Bolivian minister of defence accused the Chileans of mistreating the soldiers and President Morales decorated them,[33] thus elevating the prominence of the incident.

This overview of developments in factors determining the potential costs to militarising an inter-state dispute demonstrates that, though political–military strategies have not changed, the strategic balance and characteristics of force have both moved in a direction favouring militarisation in some parts of Latin America. We now turn to assessing the constituency's willingness to absorb the costs of militarised disputes and the leader's accountability to that constituency to complete our assessment of factors necessary for the decision to militarise.

Constituency's willingness to pay costs

Chapter One demonstrates that two factors are increasing the willingness of constituencies to pay some level of costs associated with the militarisation of disputes. Firstly, the process of political polarisation that some Latin American countries are experiencing produces a tendency to define controversial topics in terms of national interest, thereby increasing the value ascribed to them, and the willingness of constituencies to pay costs to defend those interests. Secondly, with authoritarianism a distant memory and the rise of new threats to citizen security, constituencies are more willing to support the use of state power (police and military) to address perceived threats; this is true across the region, but especially so in countries that are experiencing a resurgence of nationalist populism such as Venezuela, Bolivia, Ecuador and Nicaragua. While these two developments are occurring across the region, they become particularly relevant to the potential for militarised conflict in those cases in which a country has a dispute with another. The combination of increased value of international issues, rising domestic acceptance of costs and re-legitimisation of the use of state power can lead in some cases to domestic demands for, and support of, a government's militarisation of an international dispute.

These conditions are all in evidence in Nicaragua, which disputes maritime boundaries with Colombia and territory with Costa Rica; Bolivia, which demands that Chile provide it with a sovereign outlet to the sea; and Venezuela, which disputes boundaries with Colombia, territory with Guyana and US influence in the region. And although Ecuador does not dispute boundaries with Colombia, it continues to worry about the potential for a spillover of the Colombian civil war into Ecuador.

In those countries that are experiencing a resurgence of national populism,[34] one of the most troubling implications is its reliance on military symbolism. The fact that in the past the military often used its force against the people, particularly the same class that supports national populism, does not mean that the military has less legitimacy in a national populist regime; rather, the goal with respect to the military is to 'popularise' it, to make it serve the needs of the 'people'. But, as the military becomes a more active and overt participant in governing, issues become militarised, with the consequence that military force regains its legitimacy as a means of resolving conflict. To a significant degree, the legacy of the human-rights violations of military governments in the 1970s and 1980s had delegitimised the concept of using military force to resolve conflict. But when Morales, Correa and Chávez send the military to physically occupy property that has been nationalised or have them declare their allegiance to the new socialist project of the government, the military is seen to be acting in the service of the nation and the emotional appeal of force as a means of asserting national aspirations becomes re-legitimised. The spectacle of Bolivian troops occupying property of the Brazilian state-owned enterprise Petrobras, although then-President Lula was also on the political left, is an especially worrisome illustration of the re-legitimation of the military in populist Latin America, because it demonstrates that not even ideological friends will be spared.

The resurgence of national populism with its military symbolism indicates that the newly empowered lower classes are willing to pay high costs to achieve what they see as a resolution of national injustices, because they attach a high value to the suffering they believe was imposed upon them by anti-national forces from within and outside of the country. Thus nationalist populists believe they have borne disproportionate burdens from both domestic oligarchs and international capitalists, and that it is time to push back against this exploitation. For example, Bolivia is paying a significant economic price for pursuing a national populist strategy with regards to its potential energy exports. Bolivia is a poor country, endowed as it is with a resource (24 trillion cubic feet) of proven natural gas reserves, which could greatly improve on the US$2.9bn it generated in 2011 if the government were to provide a more stable investment climate without serial renegotiation of terms demanded from foreign companies.[35] Chile, with a stable and growing economy, would be happy to purchase gas from Bolivia, as would Mexico and the US. But the Bolivians that overthrew two governments (Gonzalo Sánchez de Lozada in 2003 and Carlos Mesa in 2005), and provide the basis of support for the Morales government, insist on using gas exports to leverage an outlet to the sea through territory Chile conquered from Bolivia and Peru over a century ago (in the War of the Pacific, 1879–1883). Bolivian governments have even gone so far as to prohibit Argentina from re-exporting Bolivian gas to Chile.[36] Since Chile will not be blackmailed into territorial concessions, Bolivia has forgone those markets and the capital investment, employment, revenue and economic spinoffs that such exports would generate. In the process, national production has stagnated, thereby significantly reducing gas exports to an Argentine government willing to pay high prices and whom the Bolivians are happy to supply.

Leader's accountability

The accountability of leadership to its constituency can work to facilitate or impede militarisation. Where leaders are accountable to their constituency, the leader is constrained by their demands – if they want a military response to an international dispute, the leader will need to provide it, but if they do not want to pay the costs of militarisation, a leader will refrain from militarisation. But, if the leader is not very accountable to a constituency because the press is generally censored or elections are tainted, the leader can choose whether to militarise depending on his personal preferences rather than on the willingness of constituencies to bear costs.

A number of Latin American democracies have been undergoing processes that not only concentrate more power in the state but also diminish the effectiveness of elections and of institutional division of power to hold presidents accountable for their policies. Part of this process of diminished accountability of leaders rests on their ability to utilise nationalist symbols and domestic polarisation to convince their constituencies that a leader who acts in their name needs to concentrate power and limit the ability of the political opposition to moderate his programme. Thus, in these nationalist populist governments (particularly Venezuela, Bolivia and Nicaragua, and less so Ecuador) one finds the dangerous combination of constituencies willing to pay high costs and leaders less constrained by their constituencies. Of course, this is not a combination unknown in other Latin America democracies. In Colombia, President Uribe enjoyed high levels of popularity even though his administration did little to improve the country's record on human-rights violations against journalists, union leaders and suspected guerrillas; this popularity continued as he increased the war effort against the guerrillas and militarised disputes with Ecuador and Venezuela. His ability to undertake these actions can be explained by the combination of his constituencies' willingness to pay the costs of confronting threats and the diminished accountability of the president. Yet Colombia differs from other cases, because Uribe served out his two terms and accepted the constitution's prohibition of a third term. In contrast, Chávez expects to remain in power as long as his health allows, after a second attempt to eliminate the constitutional limitations on unlimited re-election succeeded. In Nicaragua, Ortega has used his control of Supreme Courts to get a controversial ruling permitting his standing for a third presidential term, even though it is generally prohibited by the constitution. In March 2012, Morales was nominated by his party to stand for a third term; though the constitution prohibits three terms, Morales claims that the fact that his first term was served under the prior constitution allows him to serve two additional terms.

In a polarised domestic environment, even leaders who wish to pursue cooperative relations with neighbours with whom they have disagreements might find themselves pushed by the citizenry to require concessions as the cost of cooperation. For example, Bolivia's Sánchez de Lozada had to renege on a deal to export natural gas through Chile in 2003 a year after he had been elected president, when people rioted in the streets against his policies. In those countries where leaders are vulnerable to street demonstrations, they are also accountable to the citizenry that would riot. This power is a threat to left-, centre and right-wing politicians alike: it has seen off Ecuador's Abdalá Bucaram and Lucio Gutiérrez (1997 and 2005, respectively, who were initially lauded as left-leaning populists), Carlos Mesa 2005 in Bolivia and Jamil Mahuad 2000 in Ecuador (centrists) and Sánchez de Lozada 2003 in Bolivia (right-wing).

So contrary to common views, citizens may not be significant forces in favour of peaceful inter-state relations. In a similar upsetting of common perceptions, militaries per se are not forces that necessarily promote MIDs. Professional militaries are aware that an untimely MID, or one that goes badly, could provoke greater civilian interference in their affairs, leading to decreased organisational autonomy and perhaps reduced budgets. To the degree that the government interferes with the military leadership structure, the degree of professionalism at the top of the military hierarchy decreases, thereby lowering this constraint on militarisation. A military with some degree of professionalism might not want to militarise,[37] but the civilians (especially if they are political radicals) or civilian militia (such as in Venezuela) might not understand the dangers of militarisation. De-professionalising the military is thus a destabilising factor.

Conclusion

The militarised bargaining model highlights the five key determinants of whether a leader will find militarisation to be an appropriate response in a specific dispute. Unfortunately, in contemporary Latin America a number of these determinants have been evolving in ways that make the decision to use force more appealing to both governments and citizens.

CHAPTER THREE

Latin American hot spots

The militarised bargaining model by no means determines that conflicts will inevitably militarise, given the evolution in the domestic and international incentives for using force. But it does suggest that, were a catalysing event to develop in a number of inter-state disputes, militarisation and even war is more likely to occur than it was just a few years ago. Five areas of Latin America are particularly notable for potential sources of conflict: Colombia and its neighbours, particularly Venezuela; Nicaragua–Costa Rica; Bolivia–Chile; the Dominican Republic–Haiti; and the Falkland/Malvinas Islands. These have been explored in order of likelihood of militarisation, with a range of suggested scenarios included in each case to reflect the many variables affecting the course that militarisation may take.

Four of the five disputes with the greatest potential for militarisation are among Latin American countries, demonstrating that the principal security challenges in the region are intra-regional. Only Argentina's dispute with the United Kingdom over the Falkland/Malvinas Islands involves an extra-regional actor. (The UK also provides security guarantees to Belize, which has a dispute with Guatemala, but the two disputants have agreed to hold national referendums to send the case to the ICJ). Since 2011, the spotlight has returned to the Falklands/ Malvinas following reports that the area may have considerable hydrocarbon potential; and the British government has stated its commitment to the defence of the islands with military force if necessary.

Colombia–Ecuador, with Venezuela contributing to tensions

In March 2008 Colombia militarised its dispute with Ecuador over alleged aid to FARC; Venezuela responded to the incident by militarising its relations with Colombia. FARC and the ELN often cross the poorly marked and patrolled borders with Ecuador, Venezuela, Brazil, Peru and Panama for rest, recreation and occasional assaults against local authorities and suspected paramilitaries. Colombia has made significant progress against FARC in particular, but the guerrillas remain active and continue to receive supplies and money through Venezuela, even while that country outwardly cooperates in the pursuit of rebels – in 2010–2011 almost a dozen rebels, including FARC commander Guillermo Torres, were extradited to Colombia. In the short term at least, Chávez's ambiguous policy towards the rebels – capture some but continue to permit them to run drugs through Venezuela and get supplies – has generated increased fighting on the Colombian side as the guerrillas move some camps back into the country.[1]

The determinants of militarisation analysed in Chapter Two suggest that Colombia could engage in cross-border military actions once again and that Chávez is likely to further militarise his relationship with Colombia, despite initially improved relations with President Santos. Analysis of the factors contributing to militarisation also suggests that Correa may engage in militarised rhetoric and mobilisations, but not actual confrontation.

Political–military strategy

Uribe stepped down from the presidency in August of 2010 and was succeeded by his former defence minister, Juan Manuel Santos. Uribe had refused to negotiate with the guerrillas unless they first laid down their arms – which effectively meant he would only accept their surrender; Santos said he would not negotiate with the FARC until they had released all of the people they have kidnapped and end terrorism, the recruitment of child soldiers and drug trafficking.[2] Santos surprised everyone by pursuing a diplomatic effort to limit guerrilla access to sanctuaries, arms and money in neighbouring countries. Nevertheless, FARC and the ELN remain active and show no signs of wishing to end their armed struggle. Colombians, meanwhile, are becoming disenchanted with Santos's inability to make progress against the guerrillas: 56% believed the fight against the guerrillas was going well when Santos took office in August 2010, but the figure declined steadily and by June 2011 only 28% believed so, while 55% thought it was not going well.[3] Santos is under increasing pressure at home to make progress against the guerrillas, and in August 2011 mandated a change in military tactics to give troops greater mobility to deal with FARC hit-and-run tactics.[4] The defence minister resigned that month as well.[5] The change seems to be producing results: after the killing of FARC's commander Alfonso Cano in November 2011, approval of Santos's handling of the war rebounded to 66%. In March 2012, *Operation Sword of Honor* resulted in 33 guerrilla deaths and the capture of a FARC regional leader, just a week after rebels killed 11 government troops in an attack in the eastern province of Arauca.[6] But the fact that in a November 2011 poll 84% of Colombians believed a military victory over the guerrillas was possible suggests that delivering anything less from the military campaign would be seen as a failure.[7] Perhaps it is the high-stakes nature of the battle that has made Colombians increasingly open to the option of a negotiated settlement. A Gallup poll from early 2012 showed that 53% of people supported this type of solution.[8]

Were Santos to initiate a new militarised incident, it would likely be in pursuit of imposing a solution (a major blow or a final defeat of the guerrillas) or convincing Venezuela or Ecuador that they should collaborate with Colombia by cutting off supplies and sanctuaries for the guerrillas. *Operation Phoenix* was just such a tactic, limited to the specific guerrilla camp at which Raul Reyes was staying, in a clear warning about what might happen in the future if neighbouring countries did not limit the guerrillas' ability to relocate their camps in the face of increasing Colombian pressure.

Chávez was engaged in similar signalling to Colombia when he mobilised forces after the attack on Ecuadorian soil: he wanted Colombians to know that Venezuela would respond with force if its borders were violated. The trigger for Colombia to initiate cross-border military action in the future would be their perception that they could deliver a major blow to, or accomplish the final defeat of, the guerrillas by pursuing them across a border to their refuge; if Venezuela or Ecuador were found to be giving the rebels protection, reinforcement or supplies, that would also constitute a trigger to Colombian military action. Were Chávez to initiate an incident in the short term, it is probable he would merely be seeking to divert domestic attention from a deteriorating economic situation at home as well as attempting to keep the guerrillas from being defeated and giving the ideological right a victory (hence, keeping the dispute between Venezuela and Colombia alive). Given his medical condition, a militarised incident could also be used to claim that a US invasion was imminent and necessitate the postponement of the autumn 2012 elections.

Strategic balance

The strategic balance is ambiguous, but it probably slightly favours Colombia over Venezuela. In military terms, Colombia has the edge, in economic terms it is unclear and the diplomatic balance would move against whichever state's military forces crossed the border. Before Uribe became president and wholeheartedly accepted the US drug war strategy, Colombia's military was smaller, and had been engaged for years against FARC forces capable of holding fixed positions. But almost US$5 billion of US military and police aid between 2000 and 2008,[9] in addition to US and Israeli intelligence and training, plus a commitment by Uribe to expand the size of the army and upgrade its training and performance, have produced a more mobile and capable COIN force. FARC is by no means defeated, but its numbers have shrunk dramatically from an estimated 16,000–20,000 in 2001 to an estimated 9,000 in 2011.[10] Consequently, we can rate the Colombian military's capabilities (training, equipment, logistics and intelligence) today as high for a Latin American military.

Venezuela's military is richly funded, albeit against a background of rampant inflation. Adjusting for that inflationary pressure, and for the opacity of Venezuelan public accounts, it is still clear that Venezuela is among the highest spenders in the region, accounting in 2011 for almost 7% of the region's defence expenditure. While its spending rose in absolute terms between 2010 and 2011 from US$4.26bn to $4.38bn, in real terms, its share of regional expenditure declined by 6.4% during this period.[11] The country's military is undergoing a major shift in strategic doctrine to include a focus on asymmetric war at home to deter a US invasion. At the same time, senior officers are being replaced with politically oriented, younger officers.[12] Either change would require time and focus to ensure performance is not adversely affected, but here both are occurring in tandem.

Eight Russian-built MI-17 attack helicopters ordered in 2006 have been delivered, though it is not known whether they are ready for active deployment against Colombian forces, nor is there much verifiable data on the quality of Venezuelan pilots. Venezuelan troops, though equipped with new Kalashnikov rifles, lack the rigorous combat training and experience of Colombian troops. Although Venezuela's equipment suggests that on paper Colombia might have trouble, the latter's combat experience would give it the edge.[13] Domestic political reaction would effectively force a US president to intervene militarily in the event that Venezuelan aircraft bombed Colombia or Venezuelan ships entered the Caribbean sea off Colombia to attack.

The economic balance is not clear, since Venezuela rarely publishes statistics on the economy, and when official statistics are offered, their credibility is low. Though Venezuela's oil insulates it somewhat from the global recession, its high inflation, domestic shortages of electricity and food, and exchange-rate policy make the economy more vulnerable. Trade between Venezuela and Colombia peaked at US$7bn in 2008 and includes not only Venezuelan imports of Colombian natural gas and food, but also Colombian non-traditional exports, of which Venezuela is the largest consumer.[14] The trade is highly asymmetric, however, with Colombian exports accounting for 90% of the bilateral trade value in the first five months of 2009, just before Chávez imposed the trade ban on Colombian goods in July.

Some analysts believe that Venezuela's economy would suffer more from a bilateral deterioration of trade because of existing food shortages, high inflation and a growing fiscal deficit. Certainly, the ban on trade had an unexpected consequence for Colombia, which actually benefitted in 2009, when Chávez's ban brought down the overvalued Colombian peso, thereby making its exports cheaper.[15] Chávez uses government resources and controls to subsidise economic activity and social services to a significantly greater degree than Colombian governments, so the Venezuelans would feel the economic pinch more directly than Colombians. But over time, Colombia's economy did pay a significant cost for the embargo, with the loss of 170,000 jobs attributed to it.[16]

The diplomatic balance easily favours Venezuela, as long as Venezuelan troops do not place themselves between Colombian military and FARC/ELN troops inside Venezuela, or cross into Colombia to defend the guerrillas. We can see the impact of Latin America's unwillingness to assign blame: the publication in 2011 of evidence that Chávez has long covertly supported the guerrillas[17] barely registered in the region. However, Chávez would generate significant regional opprobrium if his military were overtly defending FARC bases. This would not mean that Colombia would receive regional diplomatic support in a conflict under such circumstances; rather, it suggests that diplomacy would demand that Venezuela, no longer able to deny knowledge of how or where FARC crossed the border, take steps to prevent future crossings. Under these circumstances, Colombia would gain its objectives even as it pledged not to violate its neighbours' territory.

Characteristics of force

The characteristics of force used in the 2008 incident reflect the fact that Colombia is already mobilised and fighting in the region, whereas Venezuela is not. The limited aims it had in crossing the Ecuadorian border and its calculation that Venezuela would not cross into its territory played a part in Colombia's decision not to mobilise additional forces to the Venezuelan border in 2008.[18] Hence, there were no mobilisation costs associated with the incident for Colombia and the effort could be easily repeated. Venezuela's response was more costly as Chávez deployed tanks, aircraft and sea forces towards the Colombian border.[19] Of course, if a militarised incident were to escalate into a serious and prolonged military engagement, both sides would face high mobilisation costs.

Constituency cost acceptance

In terms of their willingness to pay costs, Colombians elected and re-elected Uribe on a platform that rejected significant government concessions to the guerrillas in exchange for peace, and emphasised instead the need to increase military pressure on them.[20] Though Santos moderated his policy towards Chávez, no one expected Uribe's former minister of defence to take a conciliatory stance in the bilateral relationship and he won the presidential election anyway. Colombians, in short, have enthusiastically supported the increased military expenditures as well as the increased fighting. And they do not trust Chávez: in January 2008, just over a month before the militarised dispute, over 82% supported Uribe's increasingly contentious relationship with Chávez,[21] and in July 2011, a full year after warming relations between Chávez and Santos, 81% of Colombians still had a negative view of Chávez.[22] A week after the Colombian incursion into Ecuador and despite its condemnation at the regional level, 83% of Colombians supported the action.[23] We can say, therefore, that Colombians found the costs associated with this incident acceptable and may feel the same in the future.

In Venezuela, the extensive mobilisation was controversial. The only poll available is not very precise in its wording. It asks whether Venezuelans would support a war with Colombia 'for political reasons'. The vast majority, 89%, said they would oppose it. The same poll also found that 69% believed the 'Colombian guerrilla' to be a terrorist organisation,[24] suggesting that support for a conflict whose purpose was to protect FARC or the ELN would be low. But of course, further mobilisations and any actual confrontations would not be presented by Chávez as having been carried out 'for political reasons' or to support the guerrillas, but rather as a defence of Venezuelan territory and his revolutionary government against the US and its 'lapdog' Colombia.[25] Evidence suggests, however, that he would have a difficult time getting support for an attack across the border. In addition to the polling data, the people have been willing to say 'no' to Chávez even at the height of his popularity, inflicting a defeat in his December 2007 referendum to permit indefinite re-election for himself; and his popularity has been falling as the economic slowdown hits Venezuela. If Colombia were to breach its borders, however, nationalist support for a confrontation would rise, but many Venezuelans would also be concerned that Chávez's support for the guerrillas was partly responsible. Chávez supporters on the extreme left would oppose weakening the covert support for the guerrillas, as they demonstrated in 2011 when the government arrested and extradited a suspected FARC fundraiser to Colombia.[26] However, the general population has no such affinity for the rebels.

Accountability

Santos's accountability to his constituency is high, as he is just ending his first year in office and can stand for re-election to another term in three years. Colombian elections are competitive, the press is broad and able to report on the political centre, though journalists and lawyers are attacked by right-wing paramilitary forces when they report favourably on or represent unions and other issues on the left.[27] Consequently, Santos cannot expect to either keep credible opponents from the centre or the right from competing or suppress negative views. Neither FARC nor the ELN is willing to negotiate on terms that reflect Colombia's military advances. If the guerrillas continue to constitute a major security issue and Colombian intelligence locates another encampment of guerrilla leaders across the border within a year of Santos's re-election bid, the government would face incentives to attack, given the popularity of a muscular posture with the Colombian people and the comparison with Uribe.

The state of democracy in Venezuela has attracted scathing criticism, most notably from the OAS itself.[28] This has merely increased since Chávez and his followers increased pressure on the press and successful opposition candidates following his first electoral defeat in a December 2007 constitutional referendum. Although there is no fear of riots in the street yet, Chávez now confronts the possibility of losing parliamentary and even presidential elections in 2012 and thus has an immediate incentive to respond to his electoral constituency's desires[29] – which are opposed to militarisation with Colombia. But there are troubling indicators that democratic accountability will be further undermined in the future. General Henry Rangel's 2010 announcement that the army would not accept an electoral defeat of the Bolivarian Revolution was criticised by the secretary general of the OAS, a move that prompted Chávez to retaliate by accusing the OAS of interfering in Venezuelan politics, and promoting Rangel to general-in-chief.[30] In addition, when it was revealed in summer 2011 that Chávez had cancer, his brother Adán, a governor and potential successor, suggested that military force might be a legitimate means to keep the Bolivarian Revolution in power.[31] If Chávez is heading in a more authoritarian direction, the radical *chavistas* and the military will see their influence on Chávez increase. The radicals will not want the guerrillas in Colombia to be defeated, fearing the ideological and security challenges that could come from a right-wing government that successfully ended a long-standing challenge to Colombian democracy. Chávez has provided the military with a modern arsenal and economic enticements; one can assume that they will be happy to show their presence and strength as long as it does not lead to a major military confrontation that ends in their defeat. While this means Chávez will prefer to bluster, it probably also means that Venezuelan troops may be likely under certain extreme circumstances to cross the border to provide cover for guerrillas in hasty retreat, perhaps even in the name of 'humanitarian' aid.

Ecuador

A potential Colombian incursion into Ecuador follows the same logic as for the Venezuelan case. Uribe declared to Correa at the Rio Summit in 2008 and again in August 2009 that Colombia would not attack inside Ecuador again.[32] Ecuador has nonetheless reinforced its border and, at least indirectly, facilitated Colombian attacks on guerrilla forces within Colombia by making it harder for them to cross the border.[33] A Binational Border Commission (Comision Binacional de Fronteras) was created in 1996 and, after the March 2008 crisis, augmented in November 2009 with police and military representatives in an effort to improve security and build confidence between the two countries at the border.[34] Given the sympathy with which some officials in the Correa government viewed FARC,[35] however, and given Correa's increasing authoritarianism, one cannot be sure how Ecuador would respond if FARC were facing total defeat and fleeing towards its border.

If high-value targets were located and what appeared to be a major offensive against FARC were under way inside Colombia, Santos would likely be tempted to pursue guerrillas into Ecuador or threaten action if Ecuador did not demonstrate significant anti-guerrilla activities on its side. Ecuador, however, is in a much weaker position than Venezuela, so a confrontation between the two military forces is unlikely to occur. When Correa sent reinforcements to the border in response to the Colombian incursion, his political–military strategy was not to engage the Colombian military. Rather, he was highlighting the seriousness of the violation in order to dissuade Colombia from adopting it as a legitimate tactic in its arsenal against FARC, much as the Israelis have done in Lebanon and the territories administered by the Palestinian authorities. Ecuador would not cross into Colombia to save FARC because it has no strategic interest in the guerrilla group.

Strategic balance

The strategic balance favours Colombia, even as Ecuador retains its purely defensive posture, largely because the military balance favours Colombia against Ecuador. Ecuador's forces implemented an excellent defensive strategy in 1995 against Peru in a disputed section of the Andes, but they had prepared for that scenario for years and were facing a Peruvian military rent with politicisation, undermined by fighting an irregular guerrilla force that hid among the civilian population as well as in isolated rural areas (Sendero Luminoso), and overconfident because of its quick victory (under significantly more favourable conditions) against Ecuador 14 years earlier. Ecuador's military has significantly altered its situation since the March 2008 attacks: until then, while its budget had been increasing modestly year upon year, in terms of its strategy and manpower, it was focused on nation-building tasks rather than combat preparation.[36] The budget rose by 39% between 2009 and 2010, to $1.51bn, though there was no increase in 2011.[37] Equipment and training have both been enhanced (see 'characteristics of force' below).[38] Nevertheless, Colombia's military budget is more than three times as great as this, its active military personnel are more than four times as many, and its equipment and experience are vastly superior to Ecuador's.[39] Though Venezuela would surely proclaim its willingness once again to open a second front on Colombia's eastern border in the event of another clash with Ecuador, the US would surely provide Bogota with sufficient resources to maintain the military balance in Colombia's favour.

Both countries pay economic costs when their relations deteriorate. In 2007, bilateral trade was worth US$2.1bn, with almost three-quarters of that (US$1.5bn) generated by Colombian imports from Ecuador; this made Colombia the second most important trade partner for Ecuador, after the US.[40] Yet Ecuador severed trade relations for almost 21 months following the March 2008 attacks,[41] and neither side seemed to face significant economic costs as a result. Consequently, economic issues are not likely to contribute importantly to calculations by either party about the strategic balance.

The diplomatic balance easily favours Ecuador, as long as it is clear that Ecuador cannot effectively patrol the jungle frontier and does not know when or where FARC sets up refuge within its territory. Though a tacit modus vivendi between FARC and the Ecuadoran military reportedly operates at times inside the border,[42] Ecuador has dismantled FARC bases[43] and Correa warned the guerrillas publicly in April 2008 that any attempt by the group to establish itself in Ecuador would mean war.[44] But as in the Venezuelan case, if Ecuadorian troops placed themselves between Colombia and FARC bases inside Ecuador, regional and international diplomatic positions would become more negative to Ecuador. Of course, if Colombia engaged in quick strikes across the border, the diplomatic costs to it would again most likely be minimal: it would face reprisals from neither the OAS nor the US, though the Bolivarian alliance would condemn it. If such an attack were to occur prior to the

2012 Venezuelan elections, it is probable that Chávez would rhetorically condemn it but not re-impose the trade ban, given its economic costs to Venezuelan citizens – unless he were to use the incident to claim that an imminent attack on Venezuela required that elections be indefinitely postponed.

Characteristics of force

The characteristics of force of the Ecuadorian military response in 2008 was small numbers of ground forces, many of them redeployed from other points on the border. Ecuador's mobilisation costs were low. The president therefore enjoyed public support even though he had been losing support in the context of an economic crisis.[45] Ecuador signed a deal to purchase 24 *Super Tucanos* and a radar system from Brazil at a reported cost of US$270m and announced that US$57m would be allocated over three years to increase border security.[46] They subsequently cut back the Brazilian order to 18 aircraft in order to purchase 12 *Cheetah* C fighter jets from South African firm Denel Aviation (all of which have been delivered); Ecuador also acquired six *Mirage* 50s from Venezuela in 2009.[47] These border deployments increase the likelihood of confrontations with guerrillas – which would improve Ecuador's relations with Colombia and provide Ecuador with a low-cost response (they have already been paid for) to any Colombian government incursions across the border – most likely after the Colombians had left.

Constituency cost acceptance

Although no polls could be located for public opinion regarding the 2008 militarised dispute, it is unlikely that there would have been serious domestic opposition to the actual response. Since Ecuadorian troops were not protecting FARC and the response was materially moderate (certainly in comparison to the president's threat to 'pay the ultimate consequences if necessary'). But if, under the escalation scenario sketched out above, Correa ordered Ecuadorian troops to protect FARC forces and they were defeated by Colombians, Correa's government would face not only an angry military (which neither sympathises with FARC nor wishes to lose its aura of victory gained in 1995), but also domestic protests against a policy that protected a guerrilla force known to be associated with the drug trade, which Ecuadorians worry could spread into their country.

Accountability

Correa is tightly accountable to the Ecuadorian citizenry, even those who did not vote for his re-election in 2008. Riots in the street have overthrown three of his predecessors (in 1997, 2000, and 2005). His current term ends in 2013, and he is eligible to run for one more four-year term, but he has lost the support of one of his key constituencies, the Confederacion Nacionalidas Indigenas del Ecuador (CONAIE), and is being outflanked on the left by the Marxist Leninist Communist Party (MPD/PCMLE). As a result, Correa is unlikely to engage in confrontations with Colombia that carry both a high risk and the likelihood of a military defeat. Since any Ecuadorian president is bound to respond to violations of the country's sovereignty, Correa would surely respond as he did in 2008, with diplomatic protests and non-confrontational troop manoeuvres.

Nicaragua–Costa Rica

The 1858 Cañas-Jerez Treaty declared the border along the San Juan River dividing Nicaragua and Costa Rica to be the southern bank – rather than the middle of the river as generally occurs – giving Nicaragua sovereignty over the entire river and providing Costa Rica only with rights to commercial navigation. In return, Nicaragua recognised Costa Rica's 1824 annexation of Nicoya (now part of Guanacaste province). Tensions flared over Costa Rican commercial and police access to the San Juan River in 1998. Over the next seven years there were numerous militarised events and efforts to resolve the issues waxed and waned, until Costa Rica decided to submit the case to the ICJ in 2005. The ICJ decision in 2009 reiterated Costa Rican commercial rights to the river, but ruled that armed police could not use the river without Nicaraguan permission.[48]

Though Costa Rican officials do not dispute Nicaragua's sovereignty over the waterway, they object to Nicaragua's dredging project and especially to the presence of its troops on the disputed territory of Isla Portillos.[49] The question is about sovereignty, with a heavy dose of environmental concern. In October 2010, Costa Rica discovered that the Nicaraguans were clearing a channel in a disputed marshland to the north of Isla Calero, known in Costa Rica as Isla Portillos and in Nicaragua as Harbour Head.[50] Costa Rica protested at the dredging, partly in fear that a navigable route through the area would connect the two waterways on each side of the area (San Juan River to the west, with the Lagoon of Los Portillos to the east) that belong to Nicaragua and thus strengthen Nicaragua's claim to the marshland. Some Costa Rican analysts also see Nicaragua's push for sovereignty in the area as a means of strengthening its position in the maritime dispute it has with Colombia in the Caribbean,[51] and which Nicaragua militarised in 2010 (see Table 1). Costa Rica also raised concerns regarding environmental damage from the clear-cutting of trees and dredging operations, as well as the presence of Nicaraguan troops in the area, which the Costa Rican government perceived as an effort to intimidate it since the country has no military. The OAS attempted to mediate the dispute, but Nicaraguan President Daniel Ortega claimed that the organisation had no jurisdiction over territorial disputes. Costa Rica filed a claim with the ICJ in November 2010, and in

Map 2 **2010 Isla Calero dispute**

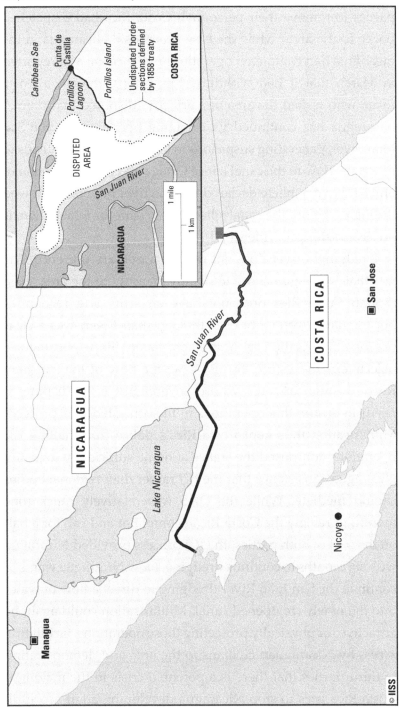

March 2011 the court issued a provisional measure for the two parties to remove their personnel (Costa Rica had dispatched police to the area) while the case proceeds.[52] Nicaragua in the meantime had completed operations in the canal, and reported in March that it had withdrawn its troops, though a Costa Rican who visited the area in April 2011 disputed that claim.[53] Nicaragua has continued its dredging operations in the San Juan River, generating suspicions in Costa Rica that it intends to divert the flow to the canal (since Ortega and other government officials have publicly declared that the river previously flowed through it before the canal silted up, a claim for which there is no clear historical evidence).[54]

Dredging a river does not require a military presence. The fact that Nicaragua chose to deploy its army to the area, even though Costa Rica does not have an army and recognises Nicaraguan sovereignty over the San Juan River, was a clear use of militarisation as a strategic tactic. Since Nicaragua's objective is to 'restore' (in its view) the flow of the San Juan River through an area whose sovereignty is in dispute, it needs to ensure that operations in the contested area proceed. Militarisation thus kept Costa Rica's police from halting the operations and raised the stakes at home sufficiently to justify Nicaragua's insistence that the ICJ rather than regional bodies should mediate. While the OAS was relatively quick (one month) to review the Costa Rican complaint and call for a halt on the part of both parties, the ICJ process provided Nicaragua with six months to continue dredging. Now Nicaragua wants to continue the San Juan River dredging to direct a flow of water into the newly (re)opened canal. Militarisation could again be attractive for physically protecting those operations, facilitating access by Nicaraguan civilians to the area and demonstrating to third parties that there is a potential crisis in the making if Costa Rica tries to stop Nicaragua developing a fait accompli as regards the sovereignty issue. At the beginning of the latest controversy in autumn 2010, Nicaragua's President Ortega declared that the UN's highest court, and not the OAS, should decide the case and that he did not want a confrontation with Costa Rica, which he accused of being 'an expansionist nation that has historically tried to negotiate what it doesn't own'.[55]

Nicaragua's political–military strategy does not contemplate a war with Costa Rica because, given the latter's lack of a military, Nicaragua would clearly be labelled the aggressor. But if Nicaragua is successful in defining the channel as the historical path of the San Juan River, it will have accomplished its goal, aided by the use of military force.

Though Costa Rica has repeatedly announced that it wishes to avoid a confrontation, in the face of Nicaraguan militarisation it has reinforced police presence on its side of the border.[56] Without an army, Costa Rica can only use its police force as a signal to third parties that Costa Rica is a victim of Nicaraguan military pressure. Costa Ricans have since the beginning of the controversy noted that their peaceful orientation requires that the regional and international community come to their aid should the country come under attack. In June 2011 the Costa Rican foreign ministry claimed that not only was the Nicaraguan army establishing a permanent presence on the San Juan River, but it was doing so to permit easy access for Nicaraguan civilians to occupy the disputed marshlands.[57]

Strategic balance

The military balance overwhelmingly favours Nicaragua as long as third parties do not come to Costa Rica's aid militarily, as the US under OAS auspices did in 1955 when Nicaraguan forces crossed into Costa Rica in support of an internal rebellion.[58] Costa Rica abolished its military in 1949 and in 1996 eliminated its Civil Guard forces, leaving it with a national police agency to carry out both law enforcement and border patrol.[59] The border-patrol forces number 2,500 for both the Nicaragua and Panama borders.[60] In response to Nicaragua's militarisation, Costa Rica has not sought to affect the military balance: the country has spent only US$1m to train and outfit an additional 153 border guards.[61] Nicaragua, on the other hand, has an army, air force and navy with a combined strength of 12,000.[62] The country's military equipment is significantly more powerful than Costa Rica's police equipment, and includes artillery and armed helicopters.[63]

In contrast to military capacity, however, the diplomatic balance favours Costa Rica. It has a reputation as a peaceful nation, having disbanded its military. Nicaragua, in contrast, has mobilised its military in the past and rejected Costa Rican efforts to resolve disagreements bilaterally. It has also rejected Cost Rica's request for mediation by the OAS in autumn 2010 and a second time after the OAS asked for the parties to withdraw from the contested area. Nicaragua insisted on bypassing the OAS and an effort by Guatemala and Mexico to mediate the dispute came to nothing.[64] Nicaragua has demanded that the ICJ rule on the dispute, knowing that such a ruling would take years. In the meantime, it has developed tactics to delay adherence to a preliminary ruling by the ICJ that required withdrawal of Nicaraguan forces from the area and provided Costa Rican environmental commissions with access to the area to evaluate environmental conditions. Nicaragua has already acted in bad faith. If militarisation recurs in the future, Nicaragua would be the likely instigator, reinforcing the perception that Costa Rica is a victim.

Of course, Nicaragua would be able to count on support from ALBA, but this alliance does not have the regional reputation of the OAS. Bringing ALBA into the dispute would suggest that this is not simply a bilateral dispute between the two countries, but is tied in with efforts of the ALBA countries to promote a revisionist agenda in the hemisphere. Consequently, an active role by ALBA would likely increase diplomatic support for Costa Rica.

In terms of the economic balance,, Nicaragua receives remittances from the roughly 200,000 illegal and legal Nicaraguan migrants to Costa Rica. A 2003 study of Costa Rica and Nicaragua suggests that about one-third of remittances received in Nicaragua are sent from Costa Rica.[65] Nicaragua, the second-poorest country in the hemisphere after Haiti, is quite vulnerable with regards to its dependence on remittances from migrants. Costa Rica is the number-one destination for Nicaraguans looking for work; these migrants are poorer and less educated than those heading to the US. Almost 14% of Nicaraguan households receive remittances from family members working in Costa Rica, and over 80% of these households use remittances to pay for basic necessities.[66]

Trade relations between the two countries are not likely to be an important factor in analysing the strategic balance between the two countries. Ex-Vice President Kevin Casas-Zamora of Costa Rica, now at the Brookings Institution, believes that if tensions worsen,

> political pressure in Costa Rica will grow to adopt harsher measures against Nicaragua, including trade-related and migration ones. This could certainly affect the burgeoning economic ties between both countries ($420 million … in 2009), which overwhelmingly are comprised of Costa Rican exports and investments.[67]

Nevertheless, trade relations between the two countries are small enough that a disruption is unlikely to affect either country very much. For example, in 2009 Costa Rican trade relations with the US were worth more than US$10bn, while Nicaragua's exports to the US were worth US$2bn in 2010, compared with US$83m exported to Costa Rica in 2009.[68]

Characteristics of force

Because Costa Rica has no military, Nicaragua can get the benefits of militarisation simply by mobilising small platoons of soldiers. The October 2010 incident was carried out with fewer than 50 soldiers. The use of its airpower or sea vessels in any operations would clearly be perceived as overkill by everyone outside Nicaragua and thus would be counterproductive to its political–military strategy. An added advantage of dispatching small numbers of soldiers is that Nicaragua can continue to claim that its purpose is to fight drug trafficking and organised crime in the area, not to affect bargaining with Costa Rica over the San Juan River.[69]

Costa Rica obviously has limited options for a militarised response. After the October 2010 incident, Costa Rica authorised the creation of a new police unit to patrol the Nicaraguan and Panamanian borders against international crime and other threats to the country's sovereignty. The new unit is comprised of 153 lightly armed men, whose training, equipment and support services cost an estimated US$1m. During the inauguration of the unit in March 2011 on the Nicaraguan border, Costa Rican President Laura Chinchilla declared that the job of the border police was to ensure that 'Costa Rica's flag will never be lowered by foreign troops'.[70]

Constituency cost acceptance

The results of a CID–Gallup poll in January 2011 showed greater worry among Costa Ricans than Nicaraguans about the October 2010 incident. In polling by Insidecostarica.com, 91% of Nicaraguans said the conflict related to unclear borders, though 73% of Costa Ricans believed that Nicaragua wished to invade it. Oddly enough, Nicaraguans believe that Costa Rica could invade Nicaragua and are apparently unaware that the country has no army, warplanes, tanks, or naval vessels suitable for military purpose.[71] As noted in the prior chapter, Ortega knows that Costa Rica does not have an army, yet claims it does in his domestic references to the conflict, undoubtedly contributing to the Nicaraguan population's mistaken beliefs on the topic.

Nicaraguans accept the use of military force to defend national sovereignty. They hold their military in high regard, partly because of a positive evaluation of the military's defence of the nation's borders – 78.4% of respondents in a recent poll evaluated the military's performance here positively.[72] The acceptance of the need to take a forceful position in defence of national sovereignty can also be gauged by the fact that Ortega's opposition in the congress and the media supported his tactics in the San Juan River controversy.[73]

In contrast, Costa Ricans are proud of the fact that they do not spend money on a military, which means that any government would have difficulty funding a significant response to Nicaragua. Costa Ricans do not want a military response, and seem grudgingly willing to fund expansion of the police.[74] Primarily, however, the society depends on third parties to defend its interests against international aggression. President Chinchilla has maintained that Costa Rica will remain fortified by 'the strength of reason and not the strength of arms'. She went on: 'We can't allow ourselves to get carried away by the profound indignation that this undeserved aggression causes us. Our tools are dialogue and international law, with those we are acting.'[75]

Accountability

Daniel Ortega and Laura Chinchilla differ dramatically on this variable in ways that suggest that Nicaragua will continue to be provocative with its military and Costa Rica reactive.

Ortega won a controversial third term in November 2011; he will not face a fourth election, unless he follows the lead of Chávez in Venezuela and abolishes the limit on terms of office. He is dominant within his party, the Frente Sandinista de Liberación Nacional (FSLN) and has created local committees that are accused of intimidating opposition partisans. The FSLN controls Congress. Ortega has appointed partisan judges to the nation's highest courts, thereby limiting the possibility that those who disagree with his policies could seek legislative or judicial redress to control his behaviour. We can conclude that he has little accountability to his constituency and thus his behaviour will reflect his own personal interests. Ortega's rise to power at the head of a coalition of groups in the FSLN, and his subsequent break from many colleagues who objected to the increasing concentration of power in his office and that of his wife, indicate that he is willing to take great risks in pursuit of his objectives. He has spoken strongly about Nicaragua's need to regain sovereignty over its historical territory both in the Caribbean (in its claim against Colombia) and along the San Juan River.[76]

In contrast to Ortega, Costa Rican President Chinchilla is both highly accountable to her constituents and highly constrained in her options. Costa Rican resources are limited and her presidency is weak. Poor choices for her ministers have resulted in four departures in key leadership roles. The 2010 elections fragmented the 57-member unicameral Legislative Assembly, leaving no party with a plurality. Chinchilla's party, the Partido Liberación Nacional (PLN), won 24 seats, the Partido Acción Ciudadana 11 seats, the

Movimiento Libertario nine seats, and the Partido Unidad Social Cristiana six seats, with four minor parties sharing the remaining seven seats.[77]

Aggravating Chinchilla's weak position, citizen concerns are rising with respect to internal security, including growing anxiety about potential threats from the Mexican drug cartels. Costa Ricans reported in the Unimer poll that security is their main concern and the desired focus of government attention. Chinchilla ran on a campaign that included taxing casinos to fund anti-crime efforts, but the tax plans were scuttled in March 2011 in hopes of a larger tax reform,[78] leaving citizens' safety concerns unaddressed, at least in the short term.

Nicaragua is unlikely to use greater military force against Costa Rica, because it would appear as an aggressor and it seems to have gotten some time to make some fundamental changes on the ground while the ICJ deliberates. If Nicaragua ultimately establishes sovereignty over Isla Calero, it will have accomplished its goal with the use of military force; and that could fuel Nicaraguan nationalism to reopen the issue of Guanacaste (the 1858 Treaty had resolved this issue). Unfortunately, the signals this case sends to Nicaragua and the region reinforces a perspective that militarisation can be a useful foreign-policy tool.

Bolivia–Chile

Bolivia has demanded a sovereign access to the sea since Chile seized its littoral province in the War of the Pacific (1879–1884). Peru also lost territory in that war to Chile and by the terms of the 1929 Treaty of Lima and Additional Protocol, if Chile were ever to cede formerly Peruvian territory, Peru would have first rights. Because Bolivia's lost territory lies to the south of Peru's, the most obvious place for Chile to compensate Bolivia lies in ex-Peruvian territory (otherwise Chile would be cut in two).

These treaty rights justified Peru's mobilisation and threat of war against Chile in 1977, when Chile and Bolivia were close to a deal in which Bolivia would receive ex-Peruvian territory.[79] Peru's position regarding maritime delimitation with Chile, although at the ICJ, complicates even a Chilean decision to grant Bolivia a free port in northern Chile, since Peru's new claims hem in the northernmost Chilean ports.

If a militarised incident were to develop between Chile and Bolivia, it could have serious consequences for regional stability. Bolivia is the leading advocate regarding indigenous rights, while Chile is active in contesting international norms granting indigenous rights, so the conflict would take on emblematic meaning in the region. If Chile were to be pressured by a third party to make concessions to Bolivia, its historical fear of being surrounded by enemies would be rekindled. Assuming the Chileans would beef up their deterrence capability in response to encirclement, an arms race could ensue.

Bolivians, for their part, feel aggrieved at the missed opportunity to recover territory (in 1977). Sentiments run so deep that a proposal by Bolivian President Sánchez de Lozada to export natural gas through Chile sparked the riots that overthrew his government in 2003. President Evo Morales has played to this strong national feeling as recently as 2010, yelling 'Patria o Muerte' (fatherland or death) after announcing that he will seek an ICJ ruling on access to the Pacific. In addition, the new constitution of 2009 promoted by Morales stipulates that Bolivia does not recognise any document that deprives it of a sovereign access to the sea;[80] which effectively means it no longer recognises the validity of the peace treaty ending the War of the Pacific. While the constitution declares that pursuit of its sovereign outlet will be through peaceful means, any Bolivian government that chooses to militarise an incident would claim that it was simply responding to Chilean

Map 3 **Bolivia and Peru: claims on Chile**

'provocations' and call for the international community to help solve the issue in the name of peace.

Many Chileans have been supportive of Bolivia's aspirations for access to the sea,[81] but few would want to cut the country in two by conceding a sovereign strip of Bolivian territory. Yet there has been no manifestation of Chilean support for compensating Peru with some territory in exchange for their acceptance of Chilean cessation to Bolivia of some of the territory seized from Peru in the War of the Pacific. Peru has said that an agreement between Chile and Bolivia is a bilateral issue, but that only holds if the compensation were with territory previously belonging to Bolivia. It would be too politically costly for any Peruvian government to acquiesce to compensation for Bolivia through formerly Peruvian territory without compensation in kind, given its own treaty rights.

The leftist Morales and centre-left Bachelet governments, like a number of their predecessors, held a series of talks on different ways by which Bolivia's desire for an outlet to the sea could be met, but did not resolve the issue. Now that Chile has a president from the right in Sebastian Piñera, the ideological differences between the Chilean and Bolivian governments will complicate any negotiations. Because Chile is in effective control of the territory and has an internationally recognised treaty ceding it the territory, Bolivia is in an exceedingly weak position to gain any access to the Pacific Ocean that provides it with any trappings of sovereignty. The Morales government appears to have become aware of this limitation in the current bilateral discussions and has sought to put pressure on Chile to be more forthcoming, by threatening to pursue the case at the ICJ. But the Piñera government has confirmed Chile's historical refusal to elevate the discussions to international organisations. It is difficult to see on what grounds the ICJ would even consider re-opening a discussion concerning the peace terms of a treaty that was signed over a century ago in 1904. Bolivia is thus unlikely to achieve satisfaction via this route.

Bolivia's frustration that it has found all peaceful resolution processes wanting could provoke a militarisation scenario. Were that to be the case, Bolivia would be likely to adopt a political–military strategy designed to provoke a crisis that would bring international pressure to bear on Chile to resolve the issue at the negotiating table. This is, actually, the strategy successfully employed by Ecuador in the mid-1990s against Peru. There are some indications that the Morales government is moving in this direction since, rather than follow Chile's lead in downplaying the June 2011 incident in which Bolivian soldiers crossed into Chile, the Bolivian minister of defence accused Chile of humiliating them and President Morales awarded them medals and promotions.[82]

Strategic balance

In the absence of a major crisis, the strategic balance overwhelmingly favours Chile, which is significantly more powerful, has a more developed economy and is a status-quo state with an internationally recognised treaty supporting its position. The Bolivian military's situation is significantly weaker than Chile's despite Chávez's support, which has enabled it to increase its capabilities on the border. Venezuela is on the opposite side of Chile's border with Bolivia and could not possibly project power there in time to make a difference. Peru and Argentina, both of whose potential for war with Chile would benefit Bolivia in a conflict scenario, are highly unlikely to put their good relations with Chile at risk for the benefit of Bolivia.

Characteristics of force

The characteristics of force Bolivia would likely use would be limited to border units provoking a Chilean militarised response. The Morales government continues to face significant opposition from the eastern provinces and thus it would not want to mobilise a significant number of units to the border in the west over the Andes. Nor would it want to risk significant casualties to Chile's significantly greater firepower and military skill. Chile is likely to respond with overwhelming force, emphasising air power, to resolve on the ground any issue before third parties could become involved.

Constituency cost acceptance

In terms of costs to constituencies, a minimal use of force would be acceptable for both countries. A Bolivian display of troops would be relatively cheap for its citizenry, especially given the strength of their feelings. The economy currently shows no signs of stress, despite the lack of investment in its major foreign-exchange earner (natural gas) because of the relative prudence of Morales's economic policies. Chávez, even with his own economic problems at home, is likely to defray some of those costs in order to save his ally Morales and his credibility with other allies (Ortega, Correa, Kirchner). Chileans would be willing to pay the small costs to deter Bolivia, especially since the reinforcement of the border has already been justified as a means of fighting transnational crime.[83] The military is well prepared for a deterrence mission and could mobilise northward without great sacrifice.

Accountability

Both presidents are accountable to their constituencies, though in the Chilean case that would most likely manifest itself in elections, not street riots, and the Chilean president cannot stand for immediate re-election, thus mitigating this constraint. Morales is severely constrained, however, since street demonstrations have overthrown presidents in recent years. So, unless Piñera takes a publicly offensive position on the issue or Morales's standing at home deteriorates dramatically, Bolivia will be unlikely to militarise this dispute. And if it does, it would be the mobilisation of forces to the border as a display, backed by strong rhetoric.

Dominican Republic–Haiti

The trigger under which the Dominican Republic–Haitian dyad could become militarised would be a significantly increased illegal Haitian migration flow across the border in the wake of the disastrous earthquake of 2010 and the slow and predictably corrupt process of rebuilding the country. Prior to the earthquake, Dominicans were already angry about Haitian illegal immigration and the increasing numbers of Dominicans with Haitian ancestry. Crime is often blamed on Haitians and there are indications of vigilante violence being perpetrated against them.[84] The periodic police round-ups of illegal migrants and the fact that the 2008 constitution does not grant Dominican citizenship to children born to those in the country illegally reflect not only that discontent, but the seriousness with which Dominicans see the issue.

The political–military strategy would be for the Dominican Republic to impose a solution to the bilateral issue. The Dominican government would seek to unilaterally prevent, or at least significantly diminish, illegal border crossings, not to negotiate or bring in a third party to pressure the Haitian government to control emigration. Given the economic and political situation of Haiti, the government has no interest in stopping that migration and is totally incapable of preventing it in any case. Deaths would probably occur in such a display of force, because of the desperation of both sides, although it would not rise to the level of the 1937 massacre of Haitians.

Strategic balance

The strategic balance is entirely in favour of the Dominicans, as the action would take place entirely on Dominican soil and in Dominican waters. Haiti has no military forces nor any ability to impose economic costs on the Dominican Republic; the UN peacekeeping force in Haiti would not cross the border to protect Haitian migrants. The Haitian government and NGOs would protest, but the international community (UN, OAS, the Caribbean Community [CARICOM], etc.) would recognise their incapacity to respond in any way. Although they could offer humanitarian aid to offset the costs of illegal migration for the Dominican Republic, the Dominicans simply do not want either Haitian refugee camps or Haitian resettlement in their country. The US government, with its own militarisation of the Mexican border and the hundreds of deaths resulting from that, would not be likely to support any sanctions on the Dominicans for their border policy.

Characteristics of force
Reinforcing the border with a Dominican military presence would be the most likely display of force should this dispute militarise; with the army deployed to the border and the navy seizing rafts and small boats.

Constituency acceptance of costs
An increased Dominican military effort against Haitian migrants would not encounter great domestic opposition. Dominicans can be expected to support militarisation of the border, despite Haitian deaths and the financial cost. The Dominican Republic scored highest among Latin American nations surveyed on their attitudes to militarisation by Latinobarómetro, with 60% believing that in a 'difficult situation it's OK to act above the law'.[85] The militarisation of the border would only occur if Dominicans perceived that illegal Haitian migration had reached crisis proportions.

Accountability
The costs of militarisation for a Dominican president are also low, considering the minimal obstacles to re-election (two

successive terms are permitted and one term out prior to seeking another set of terms). Joaquin Balanguer was elected seven times between 1960 and 1976 and President Fernandez is already serving his third term.

Argentina–United Kingdom

Argentina has never accepted that its defeat in the 1982 Falklands/Malvinas War settled the issue of sovereignty over the Islands. Malvinas is included in the 1994 constitution, with the stipulation that Argentina would act in conformity with international law to achieve sovereignty – meaning that force could be used by Argentina in self-defence. Polls at the time of the 30th anniversary of the 1982 war show that 91% of Argentines reject a military option to recover the island.[86] Though the two countries had been conducting fruitful relations on matters not including the territorial claims (known as the 'sovereignty umbrella'), the initiation of exploration for hydrocarbons in the waters around the islands has rekindled nationalist passions in Argentina and provoked new policies by the government.[87] The Argentines first declared in 2010 that vessels headed for the islands through Argentine waters must receive a permit from Argentina,[88] and subsequently have had the backing of all Latin American countries on restricting commercial activities by Falklands-flagged ships. Peru also refused to allow a British military vessel patrolling in the islands to visit a Peruvian port, though Kirchner failed to get the 2012 Summit of the Americas to take a position on the dispute.[89] Relations had generally been in decline since the early 2000s, such that it became increasingly difficult to use the sovereignty umbrella. Given the reluctance of both parties to fight each other again), the dispute will likely remain simply a diplomatic spat. But if significant hydrocarbon deposits are discovered, and particularly if the Argentine economy continues to suffer from structural weaknesses, international debt and poor public policy, the Argentine people and government will undoubtedly take extremely provocative action. It will then be up to the British authorities to decide how to respond, but they will have been put into a position with only high-cost options.

The most likely political–military strategy for the Argentines is to obstruct further exploration and production using the navy, air force, and private vessels to clog water and airspace, not to engage militarily. The immediate goal would be the freezing of activity, but with the expectation that the international community would become sufficiently concerned about the potential for overt conflict that the chorus from international institutions, Latin American governments and NGOs would force the UK to discuss the transfer of sovereignty. Former Defence Minister Liam Fox's remarks about having the military capability and will to defend the islands against Argentine pretensions have pushed militarisation back on to the agenda,[90] but for the time being, there is no need to initiate military action since the UK is in control of the islands.

Strategic balance
The strategic balance favours Argentina as long as it does not initiate violence. British military dominance in the area would be irrelevant as long as the Argentine obstructive tactics remained non-violent, and if the British were to respond with violence, they would be widely condemned and hand the Argentines a diplomatic advantage. Unlike in 1982, all Latin American countries now recognise Argentina's claims, so as long as the Argentines do not initiate an attack on a vessel in these disputed waters, it can count on regional diplomatic support (from UNASUR and ALBA). The poor state of Argentine military capabilities is a secondary factor in Argentine strategic calculations. The US and Canada will probably insist on diluting

any strong wording in the OAS. Argentina would not face economic sanctions for engaging in a diplomatic spat, though commercial activity with the UK could be negatively affected.

Characteristics of force

The characteristics of force used by Argentina would be the use of the navy and air force to clog the space around the areas thought to contain hydrocarbon reserves. The British military presence will deter attempts to actually seize ships. Argentine military vessels would undoubtedly have orders not to initiate any use of force, so the claim that Argentina would not use force to regain the islands[91] is irrelevant to this strategy. Even in 1982 the army was under orders not to harm local inhabitants during its occupation of Port Arthur, because the government understood that peaceful occupation was key to its search for international allies to promote a negotiated transfer of sovereignty. The costs of this provocative policy will therefore be mainly economic, but it is likely that countries in the region will help Argentina offset those economic costs.

Constituency cost acceptance and accountability

The Argentines will not only be willing to accept these low costs, they will demand that their government do something to stop the appropriation of Argentine hydrocarbons. Resource nationalism is a powerful sentiment in the country and, by law, although provinces can allocate concessions and receive revenues, offshore exploration and production is under federal control. If the navy and air force have insufficient presence in the waters to effectively obstruct operations by oil companies, the people will demand that Congress appropriate the funds to create a more effective military presence in the area. The accountability of Argentine leaders is high and reinforces the decision to create a diplomatic crisis. Any Argentine government that would refuse to initiate a policy of obstruction or make it effective would confront the same level of public outcry as produced by the economic crisis which led to street riots in December 2001, which produced five presidents in two weeks.

Conclusion

In these vignettes from across Latin America, we examined the key factors identified by the model discussed in Chapter Two in order to assess the likelihood of militarisation. The combination of decreased constraints and triggering events in these relationships under stress indicate that the 'objective' conditions of inter-state tensions and significantly improved capabilities have made militarisation more likely. It is therefore important to understand the strengths and weaknesses of the regional security architecture, elements of which could help drive down the incentives to militarisation of disputes.

CHAPTER FOUR

Preserving the illusion: managing conflict in Latin America

Conflict management in Latin America is focused on mitigating the impact of disputes, rather than preventing their occurrence. Prevention would mean deterring a government from the decision to militarise or working to resolve the dispute itself. However, the factors that would actually prevent conflict are not operable in the region. Security communities, such as the European Union, which have developed to the point at which the use of force is not even considered – what is known as a 'positive peace' – share a number of factors: a proscription on the use of force; economic integration at a level at which the economic costs of conflict far exceed its benefits; and a community of liberal, democratic states through which domestic political institutions demonstrate the advantage of negotiation and compromise over violent conflict. Because the region as a whole possesses none of these, prevention of conflict through positive peace is not applicable here.

In an environment characterised by 'negative peace', the expected costs of military conflict are so high that revisionist parties are afraid to engage in the use of force. In Latin America, however, there is little expectation that use of force among Latin

American states would escalate into a costly war, and there is no hegemonic power to use its military superiority to sanction militarisation, so those factors which would lead to prevention of militarised conflict through negative incentives are not operative in the region. Consequently, prevention of the use of force plays a minor role in the de facto conflict-management system, despite the diplomatic rhetoric promoting the goal of peaceful resolution of conflict.

Mitigation means limiting escalation after an initial outbreak, and bringing the conflicting sides to a point where renewed militarisation is not imminent. Since, as Chapter Two argued, militarisation is a rational decision when the benefits clearly outweigh the costs, conflict management is best thought of in terms of its ability to affect the variables that determine whether the costs associated with militarisation are acceptable to the government. The aim is to influence one or a combination of variables to the point at which militarisation is not beneficial or does not advance the desired goal.

United States: preoccupied elsewhere

Despite its military, political and economic power, for much of the twentieth century, the US had difficulty creating positive change in Latin America, even when it was fully engaged. Its unsuccessful 24-year occupation of Nicaragua (1909–33) as well as its inability to quickly halt either the Chaco War (1932–35), the Dominican massacre of thousands of Haitians in 1937, or Peru's 1941 invasion of Ecuador, are consistent with later failures during the Cold War (the Bay of Pigs invasion in 1961 and the subsequent embargo of Cuba, the domestic instability and subsequent bloody path followed by the military coup after the election of Salvador Allende in Chile, and the proxy war initiated in response to the victory of the Sandinistas in Nicaragua in 1979).

The US of the twenty-first century finds its hard and soft powers over-taxed and has fewer resources to commit to managing the hemisphere. Though the US offered ideas and rhetoric to Latin America in the 1990s, its plan for a Free Trade Area of the Americas was implemented only with Mexico, Chile, Central America (Guatemala, Honduras, El Salvador, Nicaragua, Costa Rica) and the Dominican Republic; the latest free-trade agreements to be signed with Panama and Colombia will be implemented in 2012. The only significant resources the US provided to the region were to Colombia (US$7 billion[1]) and, since 2008, to Mexico (US$2bn),[2] both under the auspices of fighting drugs and terrorism. The decision in 2008 to re-establish the US Fourth Fleet – with responsibility for the Caribbean and South Atlantic – without any ships of its own, illustrates much of the hollowness of US power projections into the region.

The focus on drugs and terrorism is also undermining US influence in the region. The US continues to view its effort to equip Colombia for its battle against drug trafficking and FARC (Plan Colombia) as a success, while most of Latin America simply sees an ongoing civil war with widespread human-rights violations by the government in the name of fighting drugs and terrorism. Venezuela and Bolivia have openly rejected militarisation and prohibition as the preferred means of dealing with the drug trade and its links to terrorism. But even more centrist politicians have dissented against the drug-war strategy, as illustrated in the report by the Latin American Initiative on Drugs and Democracy, conceived by former presidents Fernando Henrique Cardoso of Brazil, Ernesto Zedillo of Mexico and César Gaviría of Colombia.[3] After the death toll in its War on Drugs reached 40, 000, Mexico's President Felipe Calderon has begun to ask whether a new strategy, perhaps even legalisation of these drugs, is warranted;[4] Santos's position on drugs is similar. Guatemalan President Otto Pérez Molina has called for legalisation and his Central American counterparts are willing to debate the issue.[5] Thus the gap continues to widen between US perceptions and priorities and those in the region.

Whatever soft power the US has was significantly diminished when countries such as Venezuela, Brazil, Argentina and Bolivia went into economic crisis in the 1990s, despite following the prescription of the 'Washington Consensus', which advocated democracy, small governments, privatisation and free trade. The rise of Chávez and the Bolivarian Alliance directly contested US authority in the region, and even Brazil's more respectful position regarding US interests in the region came in the name of increased Latin American autonomy, which is defined as being able to decide how to behave domestically and internationally.

Despite all of these significant setbacks, the US retains influence. It played a major role, along with Brazil, in mediating a final peace agreement between Ecuador and Peru in 1998, and created the conditions for the UN stabilisation force, MINUSTAH, to be established and subsequently led by Brazil in Haiti in 2004. US diplomatic and logistics capabilities far exceeded those of Latin American countries in responding to the 2010 Haitian earthquake. The US also successfully defended the new Honduran government of Porfirio Lobo after the military coup in 2009, resulting in its reluctant acceptance by Central Americans (but for readmission to the OAS in June 2011, a third party, the president of the Dominican Republic, had to step into the negotiations). And its support of Colombia after the 2008 incursion into Ecuador facilitated Colombia's perception that it had acted legitimately in defence of its national interests. Nevertheless, the ability of the US to significantly influence the factors leading to militarisation are considerably limited by the fact that the revisionists in Venezuela, Bolivia, Ecuador, Argentina and Nicaragua are either overtly anti-US (the first two), or have made it clear that they seek greater autonomy from the US in charting national strategies for security and development.

Within this complex state of affairs, how can the US affect the levers for mitigation of conflict in Latin America? Given US unilateral behaviour in Iraq and its support of militarised strategies for fighting drugs and terrorism in the hemisphere, the US lacks legitimacy to wield the soft power of persuasion against militarisation. In the case of a stand-off between a pro- and an anti-US state, the US will have no desire to impose sanctions on a pro-US country, such as Colombia, which militarises a dispute with an anti-US state (for example, Venezuela); indeed, if the response of the anti-US state were to be sufficiently vigorous, it could to give the US cover to escalate the conflict into one that can achieve the overthrow of the anti-US government. Similarly, with a state that seems unable to control the use of its territory by international criminal organisations or terrorists (such as Ecuador, Paraguay and Guatemala), the US would have no desire to sanction a militarised incursion by a neighbour whose actions are clearly limited to eliminating identified criminals or terrorists.

Because it does not control the flow of arms into the region, the US has limited impact on the military balance aspects of the strategic balance and the characteristics of force variables. China, France, Italy and Russia are willing suppliers of weapons to the region, even providing financial and technological incentives for purchases. With high commodity prices buttressing Latin American balance sheets, the efforts by the US to limit regional arms purchases by anti-US governments through export controls are circumvented by other arms-exporting nations. And the US is itself interested in servicing the arms market of countries so long as it does not consider them to be a threat to its interests. The US could increase supplies to its allies in an attempt to maintain a favourable balance of power, but as discussed earlier, depth of weaponry matters less for a strategy to provoke a crisis than for one intending to fight a major war, which is not the issue in Latin America.

The US still has the military capability to protect an important ally against a significant attack in the region; its support of the UK in the Falklands/Malvinas War certainly aided in the recovery of the islands by the British. But Latin American conflicts are not usually black and white – Paraguay in 1932, Ecuador in 1941, Honduras in 1969 and Peru in 1995 were not important allies to the US, so even though they were subject to overt military attack by Bolivia, Peru, El Salvador and Ecuador, respectively, the US limited itself to offering 'good offices' (bilaterally or multilaterally) for a settlement to be worked out. Colombia, Chile, Costa Rica and the UK are presently allies of the US; and Venezuela, Bolivia, Nicaragua and Argentina have all had serious disagreements with the US. Even if the latter group were to engage in provocative behaviour against the former, the US would be reluctant to weigh in as a deterrent force, lest it be accused of overreacting or bullying. But if Venezuela initiated a conflict and attempted to use its naval and air power to defeat Colombia, US military assets in the Caribbean would certainly signal to Venezuela that any such use would be quickly punished by the US.

Regarding the diplomatic balance, the US is too closely identified with some actors, and too opposed to other actors, to make a difference, were a crisis to erupt between the two sides. It was, for example, unable to persuade the OAS to recognise the Lobo government; it had to depend upon a third party, the Dominican Republic, which was seen as neutral. When all players are pro-US, it could play an important mediating role, as it did in the last war between Ecuador and Peru. The US ability to influence the economic balance is also constrained by domestic politics within the US, which limits its economic carrots of aid or free-trade agreements. In addition, its actions are significantly constrained by self interest. For example, the US depends on strategic imports from some of the countries, for example, oil from Venezuela, which it has not embargoed despite serious disagreements with Chávez. The US is concerned about potential negative consequences in other areas, as well. For example, it continues to provide development aid to Nicaragua, the second poorest country in the hemisphere and a member of ALBA, because more outmigration might otherwise flow to Costa Rica and the US, heightening already existing tensions over this issue.

The US believes that promoting liberal democracy is the best means to impact constituents' acceptance of the costs of conflict and make leaders accountable to those constituencies. But as we have seen, liberal democracy is giving way to what is referred to as 'participatory democracy' (meaning majoritarian rule with little protection for minority viewpoints or an independent judiciary) in the revisionist countries, increasing nationalism there and decreasing political accountability. The remaining liberal democracies are unlikely to see participatory democracies as being bound by the same laws for dealing with disagreements, thus increasing their distrust and fear, as well as their own nations' valuations of what is at stake in the disputes. With such a perspective, liberal democratic constituents would be more willing to accept the costs of militarisation and want their leaders to see such actions as a legitimate means to defend national interests.

The result of this complex set of circumstances is that the US will weigh in on contentious issues that threaten to escalate, but not with sufficient energy to unilaterally determine when an inter-state conflict militarises and whether it escalates. The US will have to act in concert with some Latin American nations to stand a chance of helping to manage conflict within the region. A need for allies and a limited purse with which to persuade them to bear the cost of opposing the Bolivarians, combine to constrain the management capacity of the US in the region, as illustrated by its inability to come to Costa Rica's defence in the face of Nicaraguan provocations in 2009–11.

The US looks to Brazil to exercise regional leadership.[6] The idea that regional powers can be useful allies in furthering the US agenda goes back at least to US problems in Vietnam and the Nixon/Kissinger search for regional powers, including Iran under the shah, South Vietnam, and Brazil under the military government, to lend their weight to maintaining the bipolar structure of world politics. The US now seeks regional partners to help support the structure of the liberal international economic order that triumphed with the collapse of the Soviet Union but is under growing pressure. Threats come from radical states, such as Iran and Venezuela, which seek to overthrow this order; Russia, which wishes to significantly alter the structure; and China, whose ultimate goals of participation or revolution are opaque. The fact that the US is on the defensive globally, in short, means that it seeks to minimise its own involvement in a region that does not appear to raise the same serious national-security issues that it confronts elsewhere.

Brazil's paradox: global aspirations limit regional impact
Brazil has clear aspirations to be a major power and many perceive that it is becoming more active in the region. Yet a leadership role is not unprecedented for Brazil, which has participated in conflict management sporadically in the past, helping to manage Mexico's relationship with the US during the Mexican Revolution (a process which failed), and partici-

pating in the successful peace-guarantee process in the two Peruvian/Ecuador wars of the twentieth century. Brazil cannot afford to become identified as the conflict manager of the region, however, lest extra-regional states perceive it as a weak leader in its own region when an inter-state dispute develops. Therefore, in furtherance of its ambitions to be recognised as a major power in the world, Brazil has to tread carefully within the region, facilitating dialogue between parties and leading multilateral mitigation initiatives that represent minimal risk of failure. It will act only when intervention of this kind does not create bilateral tensions between Brazil and a third party.

This tension between international aspirations and regional realities bedevils Brazil in numerous areas. As of 2012, it overtook the UK to become the world's sixth-largest economy, with growth hitting 2.7% in 2011–12.[7] However, per-capita income remains just a third of that of the UK, at $11,000, meaning it ranks 100th on a purchasing-power parity scale.[8] To fuel its large economy and raise per capita wealth, it needs to ensure adequate supplies of oil and natural gas. This makes Brazil vulnerable to neighbours who supply those fuels even as it develops new resources in the risky and costly pre-salt fields offshore. In 2006, Bolivia nationalised the natural-gas output from fields operated by the Brazilian national oil company, Petrobras and, in April 2012, the Argentine province of Neuquen rescinded Petrobras's oil and gas concessions. Brazilian private investors are operating throughout the region (and globally), helped by Brazilian government agencies such as the National Development Bank (BNDES), and are running into the types of problems that have affected foreign investors from countries historically denounced as 'imperialist' (the US and the UK). For example, Brazilian construction firm Odebrecht was sued and expropriated by the Ecuadorian government in 2008 over a hydroelectric power and dam project part-financed by

BNDES;[9] and Brazilian soybean producers in Paraguay have had their lands occupied by landless peasants.

The Brazilian relationship with the US is also complicated. Brazilian leadership on the left (first Luiz Ignácio Lula da Silva, then his successor Dilma Rousseff), unlike Chávez or Morales, sees the need to work with the US if Brazil is to reach its goal of becoming a major player on the world stage. But, to benefit Brazil, the Brazil–US relationship needs to reflect some major Brazilian concerns and interests regarding climate change, the structure of the international economic regime and Brazil's goal of attaining a permanent seat on the UN Security Council (UNSC). Most importantly, the relationship must avoid any indication of Brazilian acquiescence to US imposition of its interests, which partly explained Brazil's strong insistence that President Uribe clarify to Colombia's neighbours that the agreement to provide the US with access to Colombian military bases was for domestic use only.

In an effort to artfully manage these tensions, Brazil's grand strategy articulates a regional vision of cooperation, with economic integration, political alliance and shared values (social justice, democracy and human rights) forming the basis for peaceful relations. Brazil's view of conflict management is ultimately to build confidence in order to avoid tensions. This focus, however, is balanced by a very strong non-interventionist principle, both regionally and nationally. This principle emphasises national sovereignty, and can be seen at work in Brazil's rebuffing of international efforts to influence its use of the Amazon and critique police behaviour in the favelas.

Examples of Brazil's grand strategy include the promotion of South American economic integration via Mercosur, the Amazon Treaty, and the Initiative for the Integration of Regional Infrastructure in South-America (IIRSA); the country's mediation in severe political crisis in Paraguay (1996, 1999),

Venezuela (2002), Bolivia (2003 and 2008); and its participation in and subsequent leadership of the UN peacekeeping force in Haiti beginning in 2004 and continuing today. Regarding inter-state crises, Brazil was one of four countries to mediate between Ecuador and Peru following their small war in 1995, in 2004 between Colombia and Venezuela, and in 2008 among Colombia, Venezuela and Ecuador.

Many analysts perceive that Brazil has adopted a new role as regional stabiliser, relying on 'soft power' rather than the 'hard power' typical of US and European powers at different stages in the region's history. The elements of soft power for Brazil are a long-standing professional diplomatic corps at the Foreign Ministry (known as Itamaraty), with insightful Presidential intervention at key moments (for example, amid the tension created by Bolivia's nationalisation of Petrobras assets), public and private investment and aid for the region, and a new willingness to develop solidarity with Latin America (including banning ships heading to the Malvinas Islands from Brazilian ports, if they sail under the Falklands flag[10]).

This view, however, significantly underplays the importance of Brazilian national interests in its grand strategy and overstates Brazil's soft-power assets as well as its actual role and influence within the region. In pursuit of its own national interests, Brazil prioritises national self-determination; this is, after all what it means by non-intervention. For example, as the Brazilian real gains strength on the currency-exchange market, the country is responding by favouring Brazilian products over cheaper Mercosur imports. This strategy particularly hurts Argentina, and demonstrates the primacy of Brazil's national interests, despite the rhetoric of regional integration.[11] Another instance is Brasilia's challenge and rejection in 2011 of a report by the OAS's Inter-American Commission on Human Rights (IACHR), which wanted construction of the Belo Monte dam halted until the opinions and needs of local indigenous groups were taken into account.[12] Brazil's grand strategy must not, therefore, be too deeply involved in regional mediation efforts that could force it to reveal its contending national interests.

The country's soft-power attributes are limited: Brazil has a Portuguese history, while most of its neighbours were Spanish colonies; corruption is a significant issue in the government and police; despite impressive economic growth and a major income distribution programme (Bolsa Familiar), inequality is at very high levels; internal violence, particularly in the favelas of its large cities, is significant; and with Rousseff ascending to the presidency, Brazil can no longer count on Lula's extraordinary charisma to tilt the balance. While Brazil played a role in the Colombia–Venezuela–Ecuador crisis of 2008, it did not bring it to closure; the OAS and the UN offered similar venues for the bilateral discussions that put this episode to rest. And, although the Brazilian embassy sheltered deposed Honduran President Zelaya in 2009 and insisted that a deal be worked out to return him to the country (though not the office), the main roles in resolving the issue were played by the Dominican Republic, Venezuela and Colombia. Even with respect to a Security Council seat, Brazil finds a lack of enthusiasm from some of Latin America's medium-sized powers (Group of 20 members Mexico and Argentina, as well as Venezuela and Colombia), partly out of a concern that such membership might pave the way for Brazil to play a dominant role within the region.[13]

Even Brazil's shining role in peacekeeping has been generating concern about future Brazilian commitments. Brazil's participation in MINUSTAH, the UN mission in Haiti, including its leadership, has been controversial within both the ruling party and the nation from the beginning. The mission smacks of intervention in Haitian affairs to many Brazilians and it has been accused of violating human rights. There was a suspicion that the US had promoted the overthrow of President Jean-Bertrand Aristide in 2004, which was reinforced by the fact that the peacekeeping forces did not return Aristide to office. But since the Rousseff government announced in 2011 that it will be taking its troops out of the operation, Brazil's credibility and willingness to pay the price to lead will be severely questioned.[14] Brazilian public support for an expanded Brazilian role in peacekeeping and promoting development is not assured, as many do not see a direct link between helping the region and rising as a power. Rather, they see provision of such help as a diversion of resources from those tasks that will produce international acceptance of the country's proper role in international affairs, most prominently economic development, increased social welfare and creation of an important military–industrial complex to develop a major military deterrent capacity.

A further limitation on Brazilian support for effective regional institutions may arise because the Ministry of Defence may be playing a more important role in future foreign policy, both as Brazil becomes more cognisant of its ability to use hard power and as its priorities increase in value and come under increasing attack by third parties. Climate change and indigenous cultural-survival issues have become more important topics of international organisations and conventions. The discussion of the destruction of the Amazon increasingly worries the Brazilian government, which sees the need to exploit the rainforest to (literally) fuel economic development. The discovery of massive hydrocarbon reserves in the pre-salt layers in Brazil's exclusive economic zone increases concerns about foreign interests potentially seizing control of those assets, as well as other maritime resources such as fisheries.

The sense of vulnerability in both the Amazon and the sea forms the centrepiece of Brazil's National Defence Strategy of 2008 and will surely be at the core of its Defence White Paper currently under development. The fundamentals of the 2008 Defence Strategy include non-intervention and peaceful resolution of conflicts, and no imposition of its power on other nations. It vows to defend itself not only against aggressions, but also from threats and intimidation. Two abstracts are particularly revealing on this matter: 'Capable of defending itself, Brazil will be in a position to say no when it has to say no',[15] and 'Presently, Brazil does not have any enemies. In order not to have them in the future, it is necessary to keep peace and be prepared for war.'[16]

Brazilian defence planners are preoccupied with building strong defences for the country's resources, in contrast with some of its neighbours, such as Peru, which wants to limit arms expenditures and the development of military capabilities within the region. Brazil seeks the national capacity to autonomously develop a military capability to deter great powers from seizing its resources. That includes the ability to develop nuclear weapons, but not their actual development – as former Foreign Minister Celso Amorim said in a March 2012 address explaining why the US should support a permanent Security Council seat for Brazil.[17] Indeed, the Brazilian Defence Ministry as well as industry are making significant inroads in the international arms market, including the signing of cooperative agreements that transfer technology to enable Brazilian companies to produce globally competitive military products. Brazil even held military exercises in 2008, modelling a war in which the US attempted to seize Brazil's extensive hydrocarbon reserves, which it had only recently discovered. This followed the US's decision to re-establish its Fourth Fleet (dormant for 58 years) with operations in the Caribbean and South Atlantic.[18]

Brazil's Ministry of Defence was one of the hardest-hit government departments in the review of public spending announced in February 2011: it was forced to freeze R$4.3 billion out of R$14.4bn earmarked for procurement, operations and maintenance in the original defence budget for 2011. Despite assertions that this would not affect international procurement projects, industry experts believe that some contracts will be delayed; decisions about modernisation, such as that regarding a modern fighter contract (either Rafale or F/A-18), are also slipping down the agenda. A R$19bn naval programme with French shipbuilder DCNS was spared from the cutbacks: construction has already begun on one nuclear-powered submarine and four conventionally powered, diesel-electric submarines (the first of which is due to enter service in 2017).[19]

Such a ramping up of military capacity not only runs counter to Peru's initiative to limit regional arms acquisitions, but requires technology transfers in arms purchases from current military powers such as France and China and provides the opportunity to promote domestic industries as well. A regional market for arms purchases will help those Brazilian arms producers and service providers survive and innovate. While Brazilian arms sales will enhance regional military capabilities, they will do so in a context that is expected to promote collective security with Latin American interests at its core (see discussion on UNASUR).

Despite the overt focus on extra-regional threats, the immediate potential threats to Brazil's security are primarily from non-state actors within South America. The Brazilian Amazon is vulnerable to Colombian guerrillas and transnational crime infiltrating Brazil and using it as a transit zone for the lucrative European and African markets. Brazil has taken dramatic and costly steps to repel this threat: the army initiated the SIVAM programme of airspace monitoring in 2002; a 2004 law permits the shooting down of aircraft that refuse to identify themselves[20]; and the National Strategy of Defense focuses on weapons systems and training to dissuade both regional and extra-regional threats to the Brazilian Amazon. Rousseff announced in January 2011 that the government would develop an integrated border-monitoring system (SISFRON), intended to link 33 border outposts with command centres along the country's land borders. It has allocated the project R$10bn/US$6.3bn through 2019.[21] The Brazilian air force revealed shortly afterwards that it intended to purchase low-altitude search and surveillance radar systems, as well as unmanned aerial vehicles. The government has also said it wants to double the number of Special Border Platoons, increasing the number of troops serving in them from 25,000 to 48,000. In spite of these efforts to boost its military capacity and new agreements with Bolivia and Colombia to increase vigilance along their common borders, Brazil is unlikely to be successful in significantly diminishing non-state threats in the area, given the vastness of the Amazon and the difficulty of detecting intruders. Thus it will have to deal with the implications of those threats and with South American neighbours who are apparently helpless to prevent the penetration of Brazilian space through their territory.[22] That may mean being more unilateral with neighbours – as Brazilian General José Elito Carvalho Siquiera implicitly acknowledged in boasting about Brazil's prerogatives regarding the tensions with Paraguay, an assertion of which many Paraguayans took note.[23] As Brazil faces increasing inflows from non-state actors, it will find itself confronting these issues more directly. The question is whether it will remain satisfied with the soft approaches it has historically used when Brazil's failure to resolve a situation was someone else's problem, or whether they will take a more punitive approach to gaining effective cooperation from reticent neighbours.

Those analysts who are convinced of Brazil's peaceful intentions see its strategic attitude as essentially defensive.[24] But of course, developing the power to dissuade major powers through the use of nuclear-powered submarines, sophisticated aircraft and a mobile army, is also the power to project. This in turn means having the capability to project power locally against weaker neighbours.

In the intelligence arena, neighbours may also begin to perceive Brazil as a threat. The Brazilian Intelligence Agency (ABIN) was directed to monitor domestic groups including the Movement of Rural Workers Without Land (MST), which was interacting with Paraguayan authorities. The Paraguayan strategy appeared to be aimed at obtaining the support of grass-roots Brazilian groups in negotiations between the countries to change the Treaty of Itaipu.[25]

The tensions between Brazil's global strategy for major-power status, including militarisation, and regional realities create awkward paradoxes. Historically Brazil has not included regional institutions as a major part of its foreign policy;[26] now it spearheads the development of institutions to constrain others, but not itself. Three years after it helped create UNASUR, it was the last country to ratify the treaty. Though Brazilian leaders have expressed interest in developing institutions to mitigate regional vulnerability to the global financial crisis, Brazil is not a member of the Latin American Reserve Fund (currently made up of Bolivia, Colombia, Peru, Costa Rica, Ecuador, Uruguay and Venezuela), despite the fact that its international reserves were worth US$335bn at the end of summer 2011.[27] As noted already, Brazil rejects the IACHR ruling on development of rivers in the indigenous tribal areas of the Amazon, and its 2008 National Strategy of Defense rejects the legitimacy of Brazilian citizens working with foreign NGOs in challenging government decisions for the Amazon region.

The multilaterals: going against the grain

As the report of the Fifth Defence Ministerial conference (in Santiago, 2003) put it: 'the region has gradually advanced toward a complex security system made up of a network of new and old security institutions and regimes, both collective and cooperative, of hemispheric, regional, subregional and bilateral scope, which have in practice made up a new flexible security architecture'.[28] In principle, a mature regional security architecture can impact security through norms as well as suspension of violators from the benefits of participation.

Organisation of American States

The Organisation of American States (OAS) has the strengths and weaknesses associated with being identified as a US-sponsored institution. When the US has a great deal of soft and hard power, the OAS thrives as an organisation. It was in crisis in the 1980s as Latin Americans turned against the US proxy wars in Central America and the authoritarian governments supported by the US. With the return of democracy and the Washington Consensus in the 1990s, the OAS came back into vogue, initiating the Summit of the Americas process,[29] which is an institutionalised meeting of heads of state and government to discuss major regional issues.

Though the OAS is not a security institution, it has been interested in conflict resolution and management from its inception. The American Treaty on Pacific Settlement (the Pact of Bogota, 1948) stipulated that signatories 'agree to refrain from the threat or the use of force, or from any other means of coercion for the settlement of their controversies, and to have recourse at all times to pacific procedures'.[30] Only 14 of 35 members have ratified the treaty, however. Jumping ahead to the post-Cold War era, and thanks in large part to the influence of the Rio Group[31] (whose membership was limited to democratic governments), the 1991 General Assembly of the OAS adopted an ambitious document on security, the Santiago Commitment to Democracy and the Renewal of the Inter-American System. With this declaration, the member-states took the step of using democratic standing as an indicator of whether a state could be a credible partner in the search for security and articulated a desire to renovate the OAS. Since all OAS countries (except Cuba, whose government is suspended from the organisation) were developing democratic institutions and many were worried about military coups, the defence of democracy could gain support while other potential characteristics of a security system could not. The year 2001 saw the adoption of the OAS Inter-American Democratic Charter, which defines democracy and specifies how it should be defended when it is under threat.

In Latin America, however, neither binding norms nor suspension of violators from the benefits of community participation are robust options for guiding behaviour. For example, both Venezuela and Brazil have rejected decisions by the human-rights organs of the OAS, yet faced no disciplinary action from the regional body. In another example, Chávez has certainly pushed the boundaries of the definition of democracy, violating many of the norms demanded by the OAS of member nations, such as independence of the branches of government (Article 3) and transparency in government activities (Article 4).[32] Yet the OAS has taken no action to suspend Venezuela's membership. The fact that the OAS did sanction Honduras after the 2009 military coup demonstrates that it can act. But the Honduran issue was about militaries overthrowing civilian governments, one of the few topics that unites all Latin American governments. The inability of the OAS to insist on the return of President Manuel Zelaya and the punishment of those who overthrew him, in turn, demonstrates an inability to act when the ideological and political interests of its members clash – which is the case in disputes that are militarised.

The OAS and the Summits of the Americas work together on a number of issues of concern to the hemisphere, including security. The two groups promote the development of Defence White Papers as a confidence- and security-building measure (CSBM) to decrease fear of initiation of militarisation and to promote dialogue for resolving disputes. Defence ministers meet in the Conference of Defence Ministers of the Americas created in 1995; the group is part of the organisational structure of the OAS' Inter-American Defence Board, which has little legitimacy among Latin Americans because it has historically been closely linked to the US. Defence ministers discuss CSBMs and emerging threats such as transnational organised crime and terrorism, and suggest policy recommendations promoting cooperation.[33]

With this impressive formal structure for addressing security, the OAS and its affiliated entities has experienced both success and failure. On the positive side of the scale, all Latin American countries that previously possessed anti-personnel mines have eliminated their stocks pursuant to the UN Convention on the Prohibition of the Use, Stockpiling, Production and Transfer of Anti-Personnel Mines and on Their Destruction. Peaceful resolution of conflict is promoted through the Peace Fund of the OAS, which has been utilised in five cases: Honduras–Nicaragua (1999–2007), Belize–Guatemala (2000–), El Salvador–Honduras (2003–04), Ecuador–Colombia (2008–) and Costa Rica–Nicaragua (2010). The purpose of the fund, according to the OAS, is to 'assist with defraying the inherent costs of proceedings previously agreed to by the parties concerned'. Argentina and Brazil provided experts to help implement the Civil Verification Mission in Honduras and Nicaragua. Financial support has come from Observer

Countries (Denmark, Spain, the United Kingdom, Israel and Italy) as well as from member states.[34]

In constructing effective confidence-building mechanisms, the OAS has been less successful. The Inter-American Convention on Transparency in Conventional Weapons Acquisitions, signed by member-states in 1999, has been ratified by only 15 members to date. Conspicuously absent from the list of ratifying countries are Bolivia, Colombia and the US, all of which signed the treaty and each of which is mistrusted by its neighbours.[35] In addition, the OAS is powerless in the face of the undermining of democracy in the region, nor does it involve itself productively in the Bolivian conflict with Chile over the outlet to the sea. And, as Canada noted with respect to regional CSBMs promoted by the OAS, there has been a 'lack of action … on the most serious conflict underway in the hemisphere, that in Colombia',[36] which fuels a number of inter-state tensions in the region. Though the OAS denounced Colombia's violation of Ecuador's borders in 2008, it stopped short of condemning Colombia's government for undertaking such actions, and did not address the popularity of the action within Colombia, nor the need to terminate aid to the rebels from neighbouring countries.

In a further demonstration of its paralysis in the face of member violations, though the OAS has already determined that militarisation is an unacceptable strategy, when a member does engage in it, the organisation tries not to assign responsibility. Instead, it looks for dialogue as a way to avoid escalation and, if not resolve the issue, at least demilitarise it, as evidenced by its refusal to investigate the claims presented by the outgoing Uribe government in 2010 that Venezuela had been supporting FARC and that there were still guerrilla camps in Venezuela. Therefore, the OAS contributes significantly to the moral hazard situation in Latin America regarding conflict management and has no ability to influence this variable.

The influence of the OAS on the elements that make up the strategic balance is also significantly limited. Though it used to play a role in facilitating military responses during the Cold War (such as US air support for Costa Rica in 1955, when rebels invaded the latter country with Nicaraguan aid; and after the US invaded the Dominican Republic in 1965), the OAS has no military forces of its own (nor can it muster member-support for military missions. Although the OAS has promoted CSBMs and various arms treaties, it has had no impact on the type and level of armaments being purchased in the region, nor has it affected the transparency of arms acquisition. As a result, it cannot affect the military balance in a dispute. With few economic resources, it is also limited in affecting the economic balance (the Peace Fund is for defraying the costs of mediation, not to reward peaceful resolution with development projects) and it has not been effective in promoting significant levels of economic integration between rivals. It attempts to affect the diplomatic balance by insisting on immediate cessation of hostilities and dialogue. If an initiator were seeking to maintain a high level of crisis after the initial act, OAS activities could diminish the value of militarisation to that initiator. But when international mediation is what the initiator of a militarisation seeks, the OAS actually weighs in on the positive side for militarisation by rewarding that norm violation. One can argue that the OAS has a destabilising effect on the behaviour of weaker states seeking mediation on equal terms.

The potential impact of the OAS on characteristics of force used in militarisations is also variable. Since the goal in Latin America is not to conquer one's rival, massive use of force at the initiation stage is not likely, no matter the response of the OAS. Given that the OAS will try to respond quickly with a fact-finding mission, it has the ironic impact of increasing the likelihood of significant force when a party seeks to unalterably change the situation on the ground quickly; its willingness to become involved does, however, limit the level of force with which a crisis can be initiated, and can contribute to limiting escalation. But if one of the parties is unsatisfied with these OAS-led mediations, the OAS has no ability to influence whether an actor goes to another forum immediately or re-militarises a dispute in hopes of strengthening its bargaining position.

The OAS tries to make its most important contribution to conflict management in the areas of constituency costs and the accountability of leadership. Defence of democracy is supposed to lessen fear among rival states and increase transparency regarding the costs of conflict on constituencies, and to hold leaders accountable. But the inability of the OAS to prevent, or even effectively critique the undermining of democracy by elected leaders and parties means that, in the end, it has minimal impact on these variables as well.

Unión de Naciones Suramericanas

UNASUR was created under Brazilian auspices, though it represented a broad-based regional desire for a new multilateral institution specific to Latin America. Following in the footsteps of the US-led Summits of the Americas begun in 1994, President Fernando Henrique Cardoso called the first South American Summit of Presidents and Prime Ministers in 2000. At the third Summit in 2004, the South American Community of Nations (CSN) was created with declarations for the convergence of foreign policies, infrastructure integration and economic integration via the existing South American trade groups Mercosur and the Andean Community, as well as by Chile, Guyana and Suriname. There is speculation that Brazil limited the scope to South America so as not to compete with

Mexico for leadership, and by excluding Central America, the US would not be able to use those nations as proxies by which to influence the new organisation's direction.[37]

In 2007, the decision was made to move beyond trade and economic integration issues and the organisation adopted its present name, Unión de Naciones Suramericanas, and an ambitious agenda. At its inaugural meeting in 2008, General Secretariat offices were set up in Ecuador. A South American Parliament is to be based in Bolivia, but will have little economic focus. Its announcement was accompanied with generic rhetoric about economic integration, but it will not incorporate or replace CAN/Mercosur, and the secretariat is designed to be weak; Brazil proposed a tribunal, but others rejected it. Decisions must be made by unanimous consensus; any UNASUR resolutions that are adopted must also be adopted by domestic legislation to be binding, thus safeguarding the principles of sovereignty and non-intervention in the affairs of others. Two subordinate councils were created for health and security. Despite plans for a regional bank (Banco del Sur) and a common currency, subsequently suspended in 2012 because of the problems suffered by the euro, UNASUR is driven primarily by political, not commercial, interests.

Since the institution has not developed a bureaucratic structure, despite having a general secretariat and parliament, it depends on unanimous presidential consensus (difficult in a controversial matter) to take on a case. Then it appoints an investigative/advisory team. Presidential summits are by nature politicised events, in which leaders typically make dramatic statements in order to score diplomatic points. To address that weakness, summits of ministers have been organised to focus on their area of competence, thereby reducing politicisation. The Defence Council of UNASUR, created at Brazilian instigation in the wake of the March 2008 Colombia crisis, is an example of this logic. However, when dealing with issues such as national security, it is hard to avoid politicising the matter, and impossible in a crisis atmosphere, as when a dispute has militarised.

UNASUR is an example of the 'new regionalism' in Latin America: that is, more political than economic, though still tasked with promotion of economic development. The Bolivarian Alliance for the Peoples of our Americas (ALBA), created in 2004 at Chávez's initiative, is another example and is in fact a rival to UNASUR. Both institutions are very much of the post-liberalism and Washington-Consensus era, which is to say that both seek to defend national sovereignty and give the state back its central role. But ALBA seeks to create an alternative international order working with other nations that oppose the US-constructed liberal international order (LIO); Chávez even proposed in 2003 that ALBA should have its own military forces à la NATO, but expressly excluding the US. On the other hand, UNASUR, under Brazil's leadership, seeks to use South American solidarity to achieve a better distribution of responsibilities and benefits through active participation in that LIO. Nevertheless, both Brazil and Venezuela want to control their competition, because a break with each other would clearly signal that neither could emerge as the leader in the region. Brazil also worries that Bolivarianism could be destabilising, but since it has significant roots in popular movements it cannot be eliminated; therefore Brazil believes that best path is to capture the Bolivarian movement and smooth out its rough edges. For Chávez, Brazilian leadership can keep the US at bay and give domestic forces across the region time to develop into accepting Boliviarianism where they have not.[38] Reflecting the distinct visions of its leading nations, Venezuela is a member of UNASUR, but Brazil has not joined ALBA.

UNASUR has explicitly taken on the task of promoting confidence and security among its members, as well as providing conflict management on an ad hoc basis, or as crises arise. From their perspective, this is to be accomplished via dialogue and consensus regarding behaviour. Key to UNASUR's CSBM task is the South American Defence Council. Brazil proposed the creation of such a council (without military forces) in the wake of the Colombian attacks in Ecuador in March 2008. There was initial scepticism about whether it was needed, and not just from Colombia, which worried that the Bolivarians would use the council against Colombia's fight against the guerrillas. But President Lula engaged in personal diplomacy to convince all parties that the advantages of such a forum were worthwhile. Colombia agreed to participate when Lula assured it that non-state actors using military force would be identified as a security threat.

UNASUR sees military-basing agreements as distinct from exercises; all the coastal South American countries have engaged in time-specific exercises with countries from around the world, but bases permit a non-regional country to maintain a presence from which it could attack. Thus the organisation was silent on Venezuela's 2008 military exercises with Russia, in which Russian strategic bombers landed in Venezuela and Russian warships exercised with Venezuela's navy; it also kept its own council over US military exercises with Latin American navies in the Caribbean, the Atlantic and the Pacific. However they spoke out vigorously against Colombia's announcement of providing the US with access to its military bases.

The Santiago Declaration of March 2009 (promoting the South American Defence Council) focused on defence policy, military cooperation for humanitarian and peacekeeping missions, integrating and making national defence industries complementary, providing and education and training in security matters, particularly at a centre to be established in Argentina.[39] The council regularly ratifies its complete respect for national sovereignty, the integrity and inviolability of national territories, non-intervention in the internal affairs of nations, the right of self-determination (though it does not extend this right to Falkland Islanders), and defence of democracy. In a nod towards Colombia's specific concerns, council statements reject violence by any non-state actors for whatever reason, as well as the existence of any armed non-state actors. But, also in keeping with Latin American norms regarding international institutions, the council refuses to address compliance issues. Only in the case of an overt overthrow of democracy are sanctions specifically enumerated (suspension of membership in UNASUR). Thus the council has to rely upon its powers of persuasion to convince a party to adhere to a position the council takes on an issue concerning that party; as Brazilian Foreign Minister Jobim made clear, 'it will not have obligatory decisions like in the multilateral bodies'.[40] This agreement not to enforce underlines the consensual nature of conflict-management mechanisms in the region.

Issues confronted

UNASUR could not have played a major role in mediating the Colombia–Ecuador–Venezuela tensions in March 2008, since it was not created until late May of that year. At the Summit of the Rio Group in the Dominican Republic, which was slated for the week after the Colombian attack, all members denounced the action and Uribe apologised for it. The apology was taken to be sufficient for the group to see its mediation as a success, though relations among the three countries involved would continue to be tense. At the 64th UN General Assembly in October 2009, the foreign ministers of Colombia and Ecuador agreed to re-establish commercial relations and create a working group to renew diplomatic relations, an agreement which was announced at the UNASUR meeting in February 2010.[41] UNASUR, therefore, provided the forum for the announcement, but the two countries resolved their issues bilaterally, with little input from UNASUR.

In another potentially destabilising flare-up, the Bolivian internal conflict between the indigenous highlands and eastern departments (provinces), which are dominated by the descendants of European settlers, peaked in 2008 with violence in Pando and direct threats of secession. Chávez offered military assistance to the Morales government, but the Bolivian military declared that no foreign troops would be welcomed. It is highly unlikely the armed forces would have tolerated secession, but as tensions rose, UNASUR played a major role in mediating the issue. In light of its concerns about non-interference in domestic affairs, UNASUR insisted that both parties agree to the mediation. Since the principle of territorial integrity was directly called into question by the prospect of secession, UNASUR could assume a very pro-state role in the mediation, which would be more difficult in an inter-state dispute where each party makes territorial or maritime claims. Brazil successfully insisted, contrary to the wishes of Venezuela, that the mediation effort not discuss any potential role of the US in fomenting domestic opposition to the Morales government.[42]

Internal manoeuvring within UNASUR around the issue of the military-base agreement between Colombia and the US in 2009 provides an interesting example of what happens when members' interests diverge. ALBA nations in UNASUR denounced the base agreement at the time as a provocation, but Brazil and Argentina softened UNASUR's position to one in which it wanted the US to explain its intentions to UNASUR members. A year later, however, Lula wanted to reopen the discussion of US bases as well as the reactivation of the US Fourth Fleet.[43] The UNASUR approach respected the principle of non-intervention in domestic affairs to some degree, since they were not questioning Colombia's right to sign such a treaty, but were asking for clarifications and guarantees. Colombia's President Uribe did not attend the presidential meeting of UNASUR, though he did send his defence and foreign ministers to subsequent UNASUR meetings on the topic. Uribe believed that his clarification that these were Colombian, not US, bases, and would only be used to help the Colombian government fight drug trafficking and insurgency at home, would suffice. ALBA nations, however, had no confidence in Uribe's claim; given past US behaviour, it would be difficult for any government that had tense relations with the US to accept the assertion. The US Ambassador to Colombia, William Brownfield, and subsequently Secretary of State Hillary Clinton, noted US willingness to meet with UNASUR to discuss regional issues and bring the US and South America closer together. That offer sat well with Brazil, but not with Venezuela, which wanted to press forward with denunciations of Colombia (or perhaps more aggressive action). Before plans for such a meeting could mature, however, the Colombian Supreme Court ruled that Uribe had not appropriately consulted Congress and thus the agreement was null, a ruling which terminated the issue for the present time.

UNASUR nevertheless remained engaged with the Colombia–Venezuela tensions. The organisation stepped in to defuse a diplomatic storm in July 2010, after Uribe publicly denounced Chávez's support for Colombian guerrillas. The spat initially led to a breaking of relations and tough talk by Chávez, but UNASUR's President Nestor Kirchner and Lula met repeatedly with Chávez and incoming Colombian President Santos just before the latter's inauguration in August the same year, seeking to promote dialogue in a window of opportunity as Uribe was leaving office. Santos took advantage of this opening to normalise relations with Venezuela.[44]

While discussion of the joint US bases in Colombia was still at full throttle, UNASUR's meeting in August 2009 addressing the issue ranged more broadly, including a call for a regional strategy to combat the illegal drug trade, thus recognising its critical importance for the region. Despite dissenting from the US punishment and 'war' strategies, UNASUR does not ignore the threat to individual states and regional security from the burgeoning trade.[45] Yet to date the organisation has done little to address the issue beyond recognising its existence.

The South American Defence Council also expanded its vision of threats during 2010. In the wake of that year's riots in Ecuador (by the national police protesting cuts to their pay and benefits), which the president controversially labelled as a coup attempt, the council adopted its own clause labelling the overthrow of democratic government a threat to regional security. Since UNASUR included this principle at its inception, this act by the South American Ministries of Defence was a mechanism to signal that the principle continued to be valued by the South American nations. In addition, biodiversity and the environment were recognised as requiring protection, multi-culturalism and the role of women in the defence sector were deemed worthy of study, and the defence of 'strategic' natural resources was highlighted. Significantly, the council did not include the topic of inter-state disputes as a security threat, nor did it insist on an end to threats of use of force.[46] This lack of attention to the critical issue of militarisation came shortly after Chávez put his military on alert in July and broke relations with Colombia over Uribe's accusations of Venezuelan aid to FARC,[47] a dispute which UNASUR convened an ad hoc meeting to mediate.

UNASUR agreed in 2010 to develop a confidence-building measure promoted by a number of Latin American countries and think tanks in the past: the harmonisation of defence expenditures. In early 2012, half of the member states (Argentina, Chile, Colombia, Ecuador, Paraguay and Uruguay) agreed to share information on expenditures from 2006–2010, but two of the most important countries (Venezuela and Brazil) have not yet.[48] At the 2010 meeting, Uribe's government insisted that Venezuela reveal its defence and assistance treaties with Cuba, Russia and Iran, but that does not appear to be part of what will be included in the harmonisation measures.[49] While this is an important step in developing a more useful regional security architecture, it fits into the pattern of contributing to dialogue more than addressing the actual use of force.

Continuing their pattern of downplaying the threat of militarisation, neither UNASUR nor its Defence Council offered a response to Morales and his defence minister, who in 2011 honoured soldiers who were arrested in Chile after crossing the border while armed. Bolivia's provocative behaviour around the incident, which the Chileans attempted to pass off as a mistaken border crossing, certainly undermines confidence regarding a peaceful approach to the bilateral dispute. But Bolivia's behaviour is in line with a strategy to stimulate third-party intervention in a dispute, as a means to convince a more powerful state that it should offer concessions in the name of regional peace. The fact that UNASUR has been silent regarding this behaviour demonstrates how captive its confidence-building and conflict-management efforts are to the will of the disputing parties. UNASUR is a facilitator, able to provide a context for disputants who wish to discuss their conflict, but it has no ability to cajole or insist on a discussion in which military force is not lurking in the background to be used when a party is dissatisfied with progress.

In considering the factors that lead to militarisation, and states' strategy for militarisation, UNASUR and its Defence Council reinforce the moral hazard problem, since they refuse to hold anyone accountable for disturbing regional peace through militarisation. As a matter of policy, they have no mechanisms for implementing a sanction, short of expulsion for the overthrow of a democracy. The structure of institutional governance restricts their efforts to facilitating communication among parties with shared borders where transnational crime and armed non-state actors move among nations. This strategy can diminish the possibility of surprise militarisations, by having each side aware of movements of troops and military assets, but falls short of developing a norm prohibiting militarisation.

Regarding the strategic balance, UNASUR and the South American Defence Council cannot yet affect the military balance. But if the organisation is successful where many others have failed, and its efforts to make expenditures and capabilities transparent succeed,[50] it could facilitate a better evaluation of military balance by the disputing parties, thereby making provocation by revisionist states less of a surprise. For example, Peru was unaware of Ecuadorian defence capabilities in 1995 and thus its long-standing strategy of quickly dominating any Ecuadorian militarisation failed. As a result, Ecuador gained a diplomatic victory when third parties insisted that Peru meet some of Ecuador's demands to ensure regional peace.

One might think that, by not assigning blame and insisting on peaceful discussions to resolve conflicts, UNASUR would not be affecting the diplomatic balance. But revisionist states frustrated by powerful status-quo states often want a third party to weigh in. The expectation of such mediation is, paradoxically for those who do not understand the logic of militarisation, an incentive for weaker states to militarise their disputes. To the degree that UNASUR helps stimulate regional economic integration, it could affect the economic balance among disputants by making each more dependent on the other. The infrastructure projects pushed by Brazil and promoted by IIRSA under UNASUR come to mind as an example of a strategy that could be helpful in this regard.

UNASUR's efforts to get governments to focus on transnational crime and the importance of cooperating to combat it, particularly along borders, are intended to persuade countries to invest in more mobile forces to station at the border. In fact, several Latin American countries, including Brazil, have stepped up their military presence at borders. Cooperation agreements are supposed to provide confidence that such forces are only there to confront criminals, not to pressure a neighbouring state. Yet this form of cooperation indirectly influences the characteristics of force that could be used in a crisis situation. Thus, UNASUR's recommended strategy for policing borders against illegal activity may unintentionally lead to lower costs and more proportional force when a state chooses to militarise. No longer would Chávez need to send Venezuelan tanks to the border with Colombia, as he did in March 2008, a response so disproportionate and militarily inappropriate (given mountainous terrain and the seasoned and mobile Colombian forces that were the ostensible targets), that it reduced the practical impact of his message.

Were UNASUR able to evaluate trends within South American democracies, it could affect constituency cost-acceptance, because the costs of militarisation would be transparent to Latin American publics. If it could develop a regional discourse that in fact promoted the idea of a community of nations, UNASUR could also affect the value that citizens place on nationalist-imbued issues like territory, natural resources and the inviolability of borders. Though its documents proclaim such unity, the organisation does nothing to advance it at the level of citizen perceptions. And, despite its insistence that democratic government is a requisite for membership,

UNASUR is not interested in evaluating the state of democracy within its member countries, nor has it any capabilities for doing so, nor mechanisms for implementation of sanctions short of expulsion were it to find member-states in violation. Yet as we have seen, the erosion of democracy and movement towards greater authoritarianism is imbued with nationalism, increasing the value of militarised disputes. Wherever democracy is challenged, there is a less transparent environment in which it is harder for constituents to understand the costs. Thus, UNASUR's failure to assertively reinforce its principle of democracy among its member-states represents a tremendous missed opportunity to contribute to regional stability by helping to deter the very militarisation that creates inter-state crises.

Again, were UNASUR to act on its obligations to promote and protect democracy in South America, leadership accountability to constituents would be high everywhere. Democracy, whether liberal or participatory, must hold leaders accountable to the voters through free and fair elections, a free press to inform the citizenry and an independent judiciary to ensure the rule of law. Unfortunately, UNASUR has not yet addressed the question of the physical threats to journalists and freedom of the press in South America, particularly in Colombia, Venezuela and Ecuador.[51] Its principle of non-intervention in domestic affairs has restricted its effectiveness in this critical area.

Central American Integration System

SICA was created in 1991 to reinvigorate the Central American integration process that had begun in 1951 with the Organisation of Central American States (ODECA), and includes not only the traditional states (Costa Rica, Nicaragua, Honduras, El Salvador and Guatemala) but also Panama and Belize.[52]

Like the OAS, SICA also makes the assumption that democratic government will naturally lead to peace in the region. Central America's Framework Treaty on Democratic Security in Central America explicitly addresses inter-state conflict in Title III Regional Security Article 26: '(b) Peaceful settlement of disputes, with renunciation of the threat or use of force as a means for resolving their differences. States shall refrain from any action which might aggravate conflicts or obstruct the peaceful settlement of any disputes which may arise; (c) Renunciation of the threat or use of force against the sovereignty, territorial integrity and political independence of any State in the region which is a signatory of the present Treaty'.[53] The treaty has explicit sections detailing conflict prevention and early warning measures, creating or strengthening existing Central American peaceful resolution of conflict mechanisms.

Central America has always been more integrated than South America, probably as a result of the small size of states and the fact that at independence they were joined as the United Provinces of Central America. In the 1960s, integration reached a high point in the Central American Common Market and the numerous bilateral and intra-societal organisations that developed around it. Costa Rica in particular (because it has no military) has played a major role in articulating the norm of non-recourse to force in inter-state disputes. Unfortunately, the 1969 war between El Salvador and Honduras not only disrupted the integration process, but clearly demonstrated that inter-state conflict was a serious issue in the subregion; the internationalisation of the civil wars in El Salvador and Nicaragua during the 1980s provided further evidence.

Despite the clear, high costs of inter-state conflict in the past and SICA's vision of peaceful settlement of disputes, it has been unable to instil that norm among all of its members. It thus finds itself reacting to militarisation by promoting the need for dialogue, falling into the moral-hazard trap that promotes strategies for militarisation among weak revisionist states. The organisation does not have an important influence on the strategic balance, because it neither monitors military developments in the region nor can it mobilise forces in favour of a particular party. It is also unwilling to sanction offending parties either diplomatically or with economic penalties. SICA's impact on the characteristics of force of a would-be militariser is also minimal, because all states are now moving forces to borders to deal with the drug trade that flows from Colombia to the US through the subregion. Since the goal of militarisation is not to engage other militaries in significant exchanges, these mobilisations can serve the purposes of militarising inter-state disputes, as Nicaragua demonstrated when it proclaimed that army units mobilised to disputed territory with Costa Rica were there to fight the drug trade.

SICA articulates a vision of common identity and cooperation, and thus works to lower the perceived benefits of inter-state conflict to people throughout the region. But because it has no interest or capabilities in promoting effective transparency in military expenditures or the costs of inter-state crisis, it has little impact on the constituency acceptance of costs variable. Its lack of response to Ortega's progressive undermining of democracy in Nicaragua or the attacks on journalists in Guatemala which predate the drug-gang incursion into the country[54] is indicative of its inability to influence leadership accountability. SICA's CSBM provisions were thus found ineffective in 1998–99, when the OAS had to mediate a conflict between Nicaragua and Costa Rica.[55] In 2010, Nicaragua avoided SICA and submitted the Isla Calero dispute directly to the ICJ, an action which spoke loudly to the perceived ineffectiveness of SICA (as well as the OAS, as noted above) in the area of conflict management.

Bolivarian Alliance for the Peoples of Our America

ALBA was created in 2004 by Venezuela and Cuba; it now numbers eight nations as members: Venezuela, Cuba, Bolivia, Nicaragua, Dominica, Antigua and Barbuda, Ecuador and St Vincent & the Grenadines. Honduras joined in 2008, but after the coup that disposed of President Zelaya in 2009, the newly elected government formally left ALBA in January 2010. Unlike the other regional organisations that seek to promote peace and cooperation through consensus, ALBA takes an ideological approach to conflict resolution, condemning the US and which-ever countries the ALBA leadership deems allies of the US, and asserts the right of ALBA member-countries to mobilise their militaries in order to confront serious threats. Thus, the ALBA Summit of December 2009 not only supported Venezuela's mobilisation after the basing agreement with Colombia was publicised, but 'demanded' solidarity with Venezuela.[56]

As a consequence of its ideological stance and willingness to resort to military force in 'defence' of members, ALBA is a marginal player in mediating inter-state crisis, but it could be an important actor in creating a context favouring mili-tarisation and subsequent escalation. The organisation's members include a number of the region's revisionist states (Venezuela, Bolivia and Nicaragua) but not their respective rivals (Colombia, Chile and Costa Rica). It can contribute to a member-state's strategy for militarising a dispute against a non-ALBA state, since ALBA's interest in the dispute would worry non-ALBA states that a regional crisis could develop if the target state does not offer some concessions. The military balance between ALBA and non-ALBA states could be signifi-cantly affected if Venezuela or Cuba (the only ALBA states with important military resources) were to contribute materiel or personnel to a fellow member-state in a dispute; Chávez's rhetoric promotes this solidarity, though as noted earlier, its credibility is questionable. The economic balance is targeted by ALBA, since it seeks to generate greater economic integration among its members, thus contributing to their economic benefit but not to that of their rivals. By promoting a nationalist discourse in which the military plays an important supporting role in defending the Bolivarian Revolution at home against external threats and their domestic allies, ALBA increases the willingness of constituencies to accept the costs of militarisation, both within ALBA nations and among their rivals. The value of the goal is high for both sides of the Bolivarian divide: for the 'socialists of the twenty-first century', it is to bring about the revolution; for the rivals, it is to prevent the forced imposition of the revolution in their countries. The socialism of the twenty-first century underlying the Bolivarian Revolution is driven by charismatic and authoritarian leaders (Chávez, Castro, Ortega, Morales and Correa). These leaders believe in minimal constraints on their behaviour and maximal opacity surrounding their decisions. Thus ALBA does not promote transparency and leadership accountability; rather, the organisation serves as a mouthpiece for the leaders' views, thereby affecting this variable in a manner that is conducive to militarising inter-state disputes.

Conclusion

The regional security architecture consists of two major actors, the US and Brazil, and a number of regional and subregional organisations. The US is currently constrained by its overextension elsewhere, as well as domestic discontent with foreign interventions. Brazil has its own agenda as an aspiring global actor. The result is that neither of the two major players can play the role of increasing the cost to a state that would militarise a dispute. The mantle thus falls to regional security organisations. However, these organisations are constrained by the Latin American insistence on sovereignty as the highest shared value. Hence the institutions find themselves limited to persuasion rather than enforcement. The result is that the security architecture contributes to avoiding all-out war, but creates a moral hazard that promotes low-level militarisation.

CONCLUSION

While Latin Americans continue to congratulate themselves that they are a peaceful region because of their regard for national sovereignty, non-intervention, peaceful resolution of conflict, and respect for international law, militarisation of disputes provides the rude shock that they have not, in fact, consolidated a 'zone of peace'.[1] Instead, we have an environment with little transparency, limited common understanding of threats and competing strategic views, and in which the use of low levels of military force in inter-state bargaining is considered acceptable. The only principle for the management of disputes is essentially to agree to a dialogue and no large-scale overt violent conflict. Though many Latin Americans are under the illusion that the regional security architecture is responsible for resolution of recent crises, these crises were in fact managed by other means.

The current political polarisation within a number of countries and the problem of transnational crime should raise warning flags that 'business as usual' may no longer suffice to deal with inter-state tensions in the region. In fact, the International Crisis Group and the staff at *Foreign Policy* put together a list of ten 'wars' they thought had the potential to erupt in 2012; Venezuela appears tenth on that list.[2] The situation is particularly volatile in that country: Chávez's illness, the existence of armed militias dedicated to protecting 'the revolution' in a polarised society, and domestic institutions that are losing their legitimacy raise the spectre of severe internal conflict, with great potential for regional spillover.

The US and Brazil are trying to lead using soft power because strong Latin American strong concerns about sovereignty make it difficult for a leader to emerge, and out of concern to keep leadership costs low. Both have promoted regional institutions as conflict-management structures. But as the president of the Inter-American Dialogue has concluded, 'what is striking about the hemisphere's current multilateral arrangements is the extent to which they have, on balance, underperformed. This is particularly so in light of the gravity of the shared agenda, and the expectations created in the early post-Cold War years about vigorous co-operation.'[3] Multiple and overlapping regional security institutions do not follow an institutional script when dealing with a crisis; only the International Court of Justice maintains a consistent approach to resolving a dispute. Defence consultations, in turn, do not address intra-Latin American disputes, preferring to leave those to bilateral negotiations.

Created in 2011, the Community of Latin American and Caribbean States is perceived by Bolivarians as an alternative to the OAS, and by other states in the region as a potential complement to the OAS. But whichever path it takes, it too suffers from many of the same problems limiting governance capabilities as the other organisations in the region that undermine the creation of powerful CSBMs.[4] Fundamentally, Latin America's continued emphasis on sovereignty constrains the possibility of defining key terms in line with what is necessary for confidence and security to be constructed in certain important arenas. Without defining those terms and evaluating the degree to which states are meeting their obligations under well-defined CSBMs, these security institutions can lose their relevance even while generating a great deal of press. CSBMs become irrelevant when states can either violate the agreements at low cost, or when the criteria for establishing violations are ambiguous. In addition, the power disparity in the region continues to allow the US to avoid being bound by CSBMs when it decides that fundamental national interests are at stake, and thus its Bolivarian rivals in the hemisphere feel little confidence or compulsion to follow the strictures of CSBMs themselves. Despite this troubling weakness of regional security institutions, several options for improving regional security management exist.

To successfully influence countries' strategy for the use of force within a conflict-management system, an organisation would have to ensure that militarisation of a dispute would not advance the initiator's interests. Rather, the ideal outcome would be that the initiator would find its position undermined by militarisation. For this to occur, the region would have to develop a norm that makes the use of force illegitimate not just to conquer territory, but also to affect inter-state relations. Latin America already has a norm precluding use of force to conquer territory. A norm against the use of force to affect inter-state relations would resolve the moral-hazard issue that develops when weak countries believe that they can be provocative militarily and have the regional community intervene not only to ensure that the weak country is not forced to capitulate to superior force, but also to pressure the more powerful state to make concessions as a means of ensuring peace. Alternatively, as under a collective-security system, all the other members could credibly commit to sanctioning the initiator if the target is unable to apply sufficient sanction itself.

Given the norm that use of force to conquer is not legitimate, those who would attempt to prevent militarised conflict by affecting the military balance face a difficult task: status-quo states need to have sufficient capabilities to defeat revisionists' initial military adventure, in order to dissuade them from provoking a crisis. Peru did this when it was provoked by Ecuador in 1981. To cite a more contemporary case, in the Isla Calero dispute, Nicaragua militarised that issue knowing that Costa Rica (a status-quo state) had no force on the ground that could prevent its troops from taking control of the area for the time necessary to alter the status quo. The regional community only asked Nicaragua to desist, but did not demand immediate withdrawal under the threat of being militarily dislodged by the rest of the regional community. Hence, the military balance encouraged Nicaragua to initiate militarisation. The wider strategic balance could only be affected if an outside entity could affect the military, diplomatic and economic balances facing the parties to a dispute.

Affecting the diplomatic balance for conflict-management purposes would require a regional consensus against governments that use force to promote their positions within disputes. That consensus would have to build on a community norm that rendered its first use unacceptable under any conditions, without the need for enforcement, either military or economic, by the community. Development of such responses in a particular case would depend upon diplomacy among initiator, target and the rest of the community. Without this foundation, disagreements over politics would undermine the consensus, since political allies of a party would rationalise the circumstances in which the recourse to force by their ally was pre-emptive or preventive of the rival's 'certain' use of force.

The economic balance could mitigate conflict, if economic integration were to develop to the point that significant economic harm would accrue to the parties, especially to the initiator, in the event of militarisation. Rivalry does not preclude working together on a variety of issues,[5] so we cannot take trade or common membership of international institutions as factors that will automatically preclude militarisation or limit its escalation. However, Latin American economic interdependence is not sufficient to serve as a brake on militarisation. At one end of the spectrum lie the insignificant losses that accrued to Ecuador as a result of initiating the war with Peru in 1995.[6] Yet even the level of losses experienced by Colombia in its 2010 confrontation with Venezuela did not lead it to back down in its accusations against Venezuela.

In determining what level of loss will matter in a nation's militarisation calculus, it is important to recognise that 'lost opportunities' carry significantly less weight than actual losses, because uncertainty about how the future will evolve leads actors to discount the impact of future losses. In addition, the loss is always evaluated in relationship to benefits; in the Colombia case, the government and society find themselves in a civil war with enemies who proclaim that they will overthrow the government as well as the social structure of the country; in addition, the Venezuelan government has acted in ways supportive of the guerrillas. A very high level of economic loss did not outweigh the benefits to Colombia of facing down Venezuela on this issue. In another case, Nicaragua depends heavily on remittances from its citizens working in Costa Rica. However, Costa Rica's ability to sanction Nicaragua by expelling these workers in retaliation for Nicaraguan government behaviour was handicapped, because it would have faced regional condemnation had it imposed this economic sanction, as it would have for imposing lesser sanctions (short of expulsion) on Nicaraguan workers. Hence Nicaragua did not have to factor potential economic loss into its decision to militarise the border. So the reality is that economic integration (trade and investment) has not progressed enough relative to the issues at stake in conflict-prone areas of Latin America to clearly make the cost of the use of force too high to contemplate. Even when the economic costs in a particular situation appear potentially high enough to deter militarisation, the values held by the constituency and the accountability of the leadership to their constituency, which can also affect the tipping point at which economic balance may deter militarisation of conflict, do not work against militarisation (see below).

Characteristics of force would be difficult to affect for purposes of conflict management, given that the weapons and intelligence capabilities that could be used most effectively to capture attention through militarisation are the same to which governments need access in order to combat internal rebellion and organised crime: mobility and light arms for ground forces, radar and aircraft for air forces, and ships and river craft for navies. Given the prevalence of non-state actors creating cross-border tensions, security institutions could discuss the mechanisms for greater state-to-state collaboration, including permitting 'hot pursuit' with notification.

Peru's efforts to promote arms registries as a means to dissuade arms-race dynamics would not help here, because virtually all Latin American militarisations are intended to provoke crises, not develop into a drawn out war in which resupply would be necessary. The Salvadorans, Argentines and Peruvians in 1969, 1982 and 1995, respectively, were all surprised when their military operations did not quickly result in either defeat of their opponents or bilateral diplomatic negotiations after an effective ceasefire. Since the 1941 war between Ecuador and Peru, only in the war scares of 1976–78 among first Peru, Bolivia and Chile, then between Chile and Argentina were the governments expecting a major war to develop.

Using constituencies' acceptance of cost as a means of conflict management depends on constituents first knowing the costs and secondly, deciding that the costs are too high relative to their perceptions of national-security risk. Governments that initiate militarisation will minimise costs through hiding such information or lying about it. One means to mitigate conflict, therefore, is to develop independent sources of cost estimation (including transparency in weapons purchases and incident estimations) that can operate quickly and publicise their findings, particularly within the initiating state. UNASUR is just beginning this process, which could pay off in the future. Here the international press and NGOs can play a crucial role. That still leaves the question of how costs are valued by constituents. Liberal Peace theorists argue that citizens of democracies develop norms of not using force against democratic opponents domestically, then extrapolate those norms to other democratic nations.[7] In Latin America that process has not yet occurred. But, if regional institutions could develop a sense of common identity, that might affect citizens' views about the legitimacy of using force against neighbours. However, regional political polarisation and increasing nationalism militate against this development. The value of disputed issues is increasing at the same time that mediation efforts are undermined because they raise the spectre of intervention in domestic affairs by outsiders.

Promoting liberal and effective democratic structures and processes would improve accountability of leadership to constituencies. Again, regional institutions are reluctant to pursue this, because it is fundamentally an intervention in domestic politics, a principle which virtually all Latin American nations reject. They do oppose military coups, but this is an easy and untested position to take, since Latin American governments are civilian headed and coup attempts have so far developed only from the political right. It is not clear how the region would respond if, for example, Chávez called out his army and militia and declared in the 2012 elections that the CIA had undermined the process and thus the elections had to be annulled until 'untainted' ones could be held. What is clear, based on developments to date, is that regional institutions refrain from evaluating the democratic accountability of leaders who create 'participatory democracies' that channel citizens into top-down organisations to express 'their' voice, nor do they question whether riots in the streets against government policies are true indicators of citizen preferences. Since these types of behaviours undermine the accountability of the leadership to the electorate, their development undermines the democratic constraint on using violence against other democracies.

Selected unresolved inter-state disputes in Latin America

Countries	Disputed issue
Boundary-related disputes	
Guatemala–Belize	Border demarcation
Guatemala–Honduras	Delimitation of Rio Motagua
Honduras–El Salvador–Nicaragua	ICJ ruling on Golfo de Fonseca; advises that some tripartite resolution is required
Honduras–Nicaragua	Maritime demarcation in Caribbean; migration
Nicaragua–Colombia	Territorial San Andres & Providencia Islands and consequent maritime delimitation
Honduras–Cuba	Maritime delimitation[1]
Honduras–El Salvador	Territorial: Isla de Conejo
Costa Rica–Colombia	Costa Rica waits to ratify treaty for Caribbean delimitation pending Nicaraguan claims
Colombia–Venezuela	Several points on border in dispute; migration; guerrillas; contraband, including but not limited to drugs
Venezuela–Dominica, Saint Kitts and Nevis, Saint Lucia, and Saint Vincent and the Grenadines	EEZ/continental shelf extending over eastern Caribbean
Venezuela–Guyana	Territorial: Venezuela claims more than half of Guyana
Venezuela–Dominica	Aves Islands
Brazil–Uruguay	Arroio Invernada (Arroyo de la Invernada) area of Rio Quarai (Rio Cuareim) and islands at confluence of Rio Quarai and Uruguay River
Bolivia–Chile	Territorial dispute: outlet to the Pacific
Ecuador–Peru	maritime demarcation
Chile–Peru	maritime demarcation
Argentina–United Kingdom	Territorial Malvinas/Falklands, Georgias & Sandwich Sur
Other disputes	
Panama–Colombia	Guerrilla incursions into Panama
Ecuador–Colombia	Guerrilla and drug trafficker incursions and environmental impact on Ecuador
Argentina–Uruguay	Environmental on the River Uruguay
Haiti–Dominican Republic	Migration

Memberships

	ALBA	Mercosur	UNASUR	CAN	CELAC	SICA	OAS
Argentina		X	X	A	X	O	X
Belize					X	X	X
Bolivia	X	A	X	X	X		X
Brazil		X	X	A	X	O	X
Chile		A	X	A	X	O	X
Colombia		A	X	X	X		X
Costa Rica					X	X	X
Cuba	X				X		X
Dominican Rep					X	A	X
Ecuador	X	A	X	X	X		X
El Salvador					X	X	X
Guatemala					X	X	X
Guyana			X		X		X
Haiti	O				X		X
Honduras					X	X	X
Mexico		O		I	X	O	X
Nicaragua	X				X	X	X
Panama				I	X	X	X
Paraguay		X	X	A	X		X
Peru		A	X	X	X		X
Suriname	P		X		X		X
Uruguay		X	X	A	X		X
Venezuala	X	*	X		X		X
Others	Antigua & Barbuda, St Vincent and the Granadines, and Dominica St. Lucia (P)				Antigua & Barbuda, Bahamas, Barbados, Dominica, Grenada, Jamaica, St Lucia, St Kitts and Nevis, St. Vincent and the Granadines, Trinidad & Tobago		Antigua & Barbuda, Bahamas, Barbados, Canada, Dominica, United States, Grenada, Jamaica, St Lucia, St Kitts and Nevis, St Vincent and the Granadines, Trinidad & Tobago

*awaiting ratification from Paraguay for full membership
Bold X denotes full membership; **A** denotes associate membership; **O** denotes observer status.
P denotes membership in process
I denotes invited attendee but not Observer status

Full names:
ALBA: Alianza Bolivariana para los Pueblos de Nuestra América; MERCOSUR: Mercado Común del Sur; UNASUR: Unión de Naciones Suramericanas; CAN: Comunidad Andina ; CELAC: Comunidad de Estados Latinoamericanos y Caribeños ; SICA: Sistema de la Integración Centroamericana; OAS: Organización de los Estados Americanos

APPENDIX THREE

Latin America boundary settlements 2000–2011

Costa Rica–Colombia 2000	Maritime boundaries in Pacific Ocean (bilateral)
Peru–Chile 2000	Final implementation of 1929 territorial agreement (bilateral)
Honduras–El Salvador 2003	Land, island and maritime (ICJ reaffirm 1992 decision)
Honduras–Nicaragua 2007	Maritime, ICJ
Nicaragua–Costa Rica 2009	Riverine access, ICJ
Venezuela–Trinidad & Tobago 2010	Maritime boundaries (bilateral)
Argentina–Uruguay 2010	Environmental, ICJ
In process	
Nicaragua–Colombia	At the ICJ (territorial and maritime delimitation)
Peru–Chile	At the ICJ (maritime delimitation)
Ecuador–Colombia	At the ICJ (environmental)
Costa Rica–Nicaragua	At the ICJ (territorial and environmental)
Guatemala–Belize	At OAS/to be sent to ICJ (territorial)

NOTES

Introduction

1   Gabriel Marcella, *War Without Borders: The Colombia–Ecuador Crisis of 2008* (Carlisle, PA: Strategic Studies Institute, US Army War College, 2008) ,p. 5

2   The incursion took place on 1 March 2008. Venezuela and Ecuador moved troops to their borders a day later, while Colombia insisted it had been pursuing terrorists who had kidnapped and killed many thousands of Colombian citizens. As the diplomatic crisis deepened, Bogotá said it had seized secret files during the raid, on a laptop belonging to FARC leader Raúl Reyes, who was among 17 rebels killed in the attack. The Colombians claimed these files showed that Chávez had given funding to FARC, and that the group was being given shelter in Venezuela with Chávez's knowledge. At a summit of the Rio Group held in the Dominican Republic on 7 March, the three leaders agreed to end the crisis, but Colombia and Ecuador did not restore full diplomatic relations until November 2010.

3   13% of MIDs begin with a threat to use force; 38% initiate with a display of force; and 49% erupt with outright use of force without prior threat or display. The level of MID does not dictate the level of the response: 47% of threats are responded to with threats, 59% of displays result in reciprocal displays, and use of force provokes a similar response 43% of the time. Charles S. Gochman and Zeev Maoz, 'Militarized Interstate Disputes, 1816–1976', *Journal of Conflict Resolution*, vol. 28, no. 4, December 1984, pp. 606–9.

4   'UK Committed to Falklands in Spite of all the "Huff and Puff" from Argentine Politicians', *MercoPress*, 27 June 2011, http://en.mercopress.com/2011/06/27/uk-committed-to-falklands-in-spite-of-all-the-huff-and-puff-from-argentine-politicians.

5   Thomas Harding, 'HMS Dauntless Sets Sail for Falklands as Tensions Mount between Britain and Argentina', *Telegraph*, 4 Apr 2012; Thomas Harding, 'Argentina to Invade Falklands after 30th Anniversary Furore Dies Down, Commander Warns', *Telegraph*, 12 April 2012.

6   David R. Mares and David Scott Palmer, *Institutions, Power, and Leadership in War and Peace: Lessons from*

Peru and Ecuador, 1995–1998 (Austin, TX: University of Texas Press, 2012).

7   See http://www.correlatesofwar.org/; Daniel M. Jones, Stuart A. Bremer and J. David Singer, 'Militarized Interstate Disputes, 1816–1992: Rationale, Coding Rules, and Empirical Patterns', *Conflict Management and Peace Studies*, vol. 15, no. 2, 1996, pp. 163–212.

8   Lack of investment has seriously limited both Argentine and Bolivian natural-gas exports to their neighbours, undermining much of the confidence-building constructed around energy integration. See Augusto Varas, Claudio Fuentes and Felipe Agüero, *Instituciones Cautivas: Opinión pública y nueva legitimidad social de las Fuerzas Armadas* (Santiago, Chile: FLACSO, 2007), p. 66.

9   David Pion-Berlin and Harold Trinkunas, 'Civilian Praetorianism and Military Shirking during Constitutional Crises in Latin America', *Comparative Politics*, vol. 42, no. 4, July 2010, pp. 395–411.

10 *The Military Balance 1987/88* (London: Routledge for IISS), pp. 182–8; *The Military Balance 1997/98*, pp. 209–16. Ecuador brought inflation down from a staggering 11,980% in 1985 to 276% the year after; during this period the country's defence budget fell from $245.85m to $166.15m.

11 Arie Kacowicz, *Zones of Peace in the Third World: South America and West Africa in Comparative Perspective* (Albany, NY: State University of New York 1998); David R. Mares, *Violent Peace* (New York: Columbia University Press, 2001).

12 Jorge Castañeda, *Utopia Unarmed: The Latin American Left after the Cold War* (New York: Vintage, 1993).

13 See William R. Cohen, *Report of the Secretary of Defense to the President and the Congress*, Office of the Secretary of Defense, Washington DC, 2000, pp. 12, 179.

14 Michelle Bachelet Jeria, 'Fifth Conference of Ministers of Defense of the Americas. Report of the Outgoing Chair', Committee on Hemispheric Security, OEA/Ser.G. CP/CSH/INF. 19/03 add., 1 February 25, 2003, p. 4.

15 Richard J. Bloomfield and P. Lincoln, 'Meeting of Experts on Confidence and Security Building Measures', Remarks to Organization of American States Summit-Mandated Meeting of Experts on CSBMs, Miami, 3 February 2003, as cited in David R. Mares, 'Confidence- and Security-Building Measures: Relevance and Efficiency', in Gordon Mace, Jean-Philippe Therien and Paul Haslam (eds), *Governing the Americas: Assessing Multilateral Institutions* (Boulder, CO: Lynne Rienner Publishers, 2007), p. 106.

16 See address by the SICA president 'Discurso del Secretario General del SICA, Doctor Juan Daniel Alemán Gurdián, en ocasión de la Conferencia Internacional de Apoyo a la Estrategia de Seguridad de Centroamérica', http://www.sica.int/busqueda/Noticias.aspx?IDItem=60497&IDCat=3&IdEnt=1&Idm=1&IdmStyle=1.

17 Allan R. Brewer-Carías, *Dismantling Democracy in Venezuela: The Chávez Authoritarian Experiment* (New York: Cambridge University Press, 2010).

18 John Crabtree, 'Bolivia's Controversial Constitution', *OpenDemocracy*, 10 December 2007, http://www.opendemocracy.net/article/bolivia_s_controversial_constitution.

19 Tim Rogers, 'Why Nicaragua's Capital Is in Flames', Time.com, 14 November 2008, http://www.time.com/time/world/article/0,8599,1858920,00.html#ixzz1hmhR7vte.

20 Brewer-Carias, *Dismantling Democracy.*

21 'Argentina Calls on Mercosur To Promote Inter-trade and Cut out of Region Imports', MercoPress, 13 October 2011, http://en.mercopress. com/2011/10/13/argentina-calls-on-mercosur-to-promote-inter-trade-and-cut-out-of-region-imports.

22 'Central America economic integration: Advances and perspectives', Inter-American Development Bank 23 September 2011, http://idbdocs.

iadb.org/wsdocs/getdocument. aspx?docnum=36428027.

23 Vello Kuuskraa et. al., 'World Shale Gas Resources: An Initial Assessment of 14 Regions Outside the United States' (Arlington, VA: Advanced Resources International, Inc., April 2011).

24 Daniel Yergin and James Burkhard, 'The Great Revival: The Western Hemisphere's Oil Renaissance', *Wall Street Journal*, 6 March 2012, http://online.wsj.com/ad/article/ceraweek2012-revival.

Chapter One

1 Robert L. Scheina, *History of Latin America's Wars*, vol. 2 (Dulles, VA: Brassey's, 2003).

2 'Peru Accepts Ecuador Maritime Borders, Much to Chile's Chagrin', MercoPress, 4 May 2011.

3 Daniel Ok, 'Bolivia/Chile Pacific Access', Council on Hemispheric Affairs, 24 June 2011, http://www.coha. org/boliviachile-pacific-access/.

4 Leo Palmer, 'Nicaragua Threatens Military Action Against Colombia', *Colombia Reports*, 26 July 2010, http:// colombiareports.com/colombia-news/ news/10999-nicaragua-threatens-military-action-against-colombia.html.

5 This was the justification for many of the military-run 'national security states' of the 1960s and 1970s.

6 The International Institute for Strategic Studies, *The FARC Files: Venezuela, Ecuador and the Secret Archive of 'Raúl Reyes'* (London: IISS, 2011).

7 Michael Shifter, 'The Chávezjad Doctrine: Between Myth and Speculation', *Poder*, 5 January 2010.

8 Cynthia Arnson, Haleh Esfandiari, and Adam Stubits (eds), *Iran in Latin America: Threat or 'Axis of Annoyance'?* (Washington, DC: Woodrow Wilson International Center for Scholars, n.d.).

9 Robin Yapp, 'Iran Defence Minister Forced to Leave Bolivia over 1994 Argentina Bombing', *Telegraph*, 1 June 2011.

10 Matthew Stabley, 'Iranian Faction Plotted to Kill Saudi Ambassador: Holder', NBC Washington, 13 October 2011.

11 See the accusations of Iranian terrorist links, including some made by former US government officials, at www. InterAmericanSecurityWatch.com.

12 Peter Griffiths, 'UK's Brown Says Talks will End Falklands Oil Row', Reuters, 18 February 2010.

13 'Caracas, Trinidad Reach Border Fields Accord', *Oil & Gas Journal*, 12 March 2007, p. 8.

14 'Brazil's Oil Boom: Filling Up the Future', *Economist*, 5 November

2011, http://www.economist.com/node/21536570.

15 *The Military Balance 2012*, p. 367.

16 Augusto Varas, Claudio Fuentes y Felipe Agüero, *Instituciones cautivas. Opinión pública y nueva legitimidad social de las Fuerzas Armadas* (Santiago: FLACSO-Catalonia, 2008), p. 66.

17 Bolivia lost territory on three occasions. In 1883, as a consequence of its defeat by Chile in the War of the Pacific (1879–83), Bolivia lost its maritime province, and with it significant wealth generated by the guano deposits. Between 1899 and 1903, Bolivia's central government forces skirmished with Brazilian adventurers seeking to lay claim to the rubber-rich Acre province, but were forced to sell the territory when Brazil dispatched troops to the area. In the Chaco War (1932–35) 65,000 Bolivians were killed and the country lost US$200 million and its claim to extensive territory, mistakenly believed to have large oil deposits, to Paraguay. See. Mares, *Violent Peace*, pp. 62–72.

18 Raúl Zibechi, 'Ecuador: The Battle for Natural Resources Deepens', Americas Program, Center for International Policy, 26 October 2009, available at http://www.americas.irc-online.com.

19 International Court of Justice, 'Summary of the Judgment of 13 December 2007, Territorial and Maritime Dispute (Nicaragua v. Colombia), Preliminary Objections', http://www.icj-cij.org/docket/files/124/14325.pdf.

20 'Peru–Chile Border Row Escalates', BBC News, 4 November 2005; Simon Romero, 'Peru: Officer Says He Spied For Chile', *New York Times*, 18 November 2009, p. A 8.

21 Diego González, 'Lugo's Dilemmas', Americas Program, Center for International Policy, 26 September 2009, available at http://www.americas.irc-online.com; 'Senate Approves Payment Rise for Itaipu Energy', Government of Brazil, Senado Federal, *Portal de Noticias*, 13 May 2011, www.senado.gov.br/noticias/agencia/internacional/en/not_1293.aspx.

22 Raúl Zibechi, 'Is Brazil Creating Its Own "Backyard"?', *Zibechi Report*, no. 12, 3 February 2009, Americas Program, Center for International Policy, available at http://www.americas.irc-online.com; see 'US Embassy Cables: Washington Worries that Paraguay Harbours Iranian Agents and Islamist Terrorists', *Guardian*, 28 October 2010, http://www.guardian.co.uk/world/us-embassy-cables-documents/147040..

23 *Ibid.*; Kelly Hearn, 'China Plants Bitter Seeds in South American Farmland', *Washington Times*, 1 February 2012.

24 Raúl Zibechi, 'The Soybean Crop in Uruguay: The Creation of a Power Block', Americas Program, Center for International Policy, 8 July 2007, available at http://www.americas.irc-online.com.

25 Sara Miller Llana, 'Across Much of Latin America, Inflation is the Top Issue', *Christian Science Monitor* 20 May 2008, p. 6.

26 Kari Hamerschlag, 'The Bolivia–Brazil Pipeline: A "Model" Project?', Bank Information Center, 10 December 2003, http://www.bicusa.org/en/Article.454.aspx.

27 Zeibechi, 'Is Brazil Creating Its Own "Backyard"?'.

28 Sean Johnson, 'Venezuela–Colombia Relations in Limbo: Will Chávez Burn the Bridge?', Council On Hemispheric Affairs, 7 August 2009.

29 US Department of State, *International Narcotics Control Strategy Report* 2009, 'Mexico II: Status of Country', p. 414, http://www.state.gov/documents/organization/120054.pdf.

30 Richard A. Serrano, 'Guns from U.S. Equip Drug Cartels', *Los Angeles Times*, 10 August 2008.

31 Rachel Stohl and Doug Tuttle, 'Small Arms Trade in Latin America', *NACLA Report on the Americas*, March–April 2008, p. 20.

32 .Juan O. Tamayo, 'FARC Rebels' Missile Purchase Raises Concerns', *Miami Herald*, 16 February 2010.

33 Kaitlin Porter, 'Stateless in the Dominican Republic', Council On Hemispheric Affairs, 12 August 2009.

34 Juan Forero, 'Another Bump in a Rocky Road for Colombia and Venezuela', *New York Times*, 30 November 2000, p. A12.

35 Laura Carlsen, 'Mexico's Immigration Problem also a "Red Flag" at Home', Americas Program, 3 December 2008; Suzana Shepard-Durni, 'Mexico's Other Border: Issues Affecting Mexico's Dividing Line with Guatemala', Council On Hemispheric Affairs, 12 September 2008.

36 'General: Peru Formally Presents Its Ocean-Borders Case Against Chile at The Hague', *NotiSur*, 2 August 2008.

37 .Cristina Albertin, 'Encountering Human Trafficking in Bolivia' (Geneva: United Nations Office on Drugs and Crime, 9 June 2008), http://www.unodc.org/unodc/en/frontpage/encountering-human-trafficking-in-bolivia.html.

38 Latin American Economic System, *Migrations and Remittances in Latin America and the Caribbean: Intra-regional Flows and Macroeconomic Determinants* (Caracas: SELA Secretariat, 2005).

39 Stephen Johnson and David B. Muhlhausen, 'North American Transnational Youth Gangs: Breaking the Chain of Violence', *Backgrounder*, No. 1834, *The Heritage Foundation*, 21 March 2005; Leah Chavla, 'FARQaeda* (FARC + Al Qaeda): A Real Threat or a Matter of Circumstantial Evidence?', Council on Hemispheric Affairs, 3 February 2010.

40 There is a great deal of scepticism concerning the alleged plot. Sara Miller Llana, 'Iran Assassination Plot: Terrorists Join Forces with Mexican Drug Cartels?', *Christian Science Monitor*, 11 October 2011.

41 Univision, 'La Amenaza Iraní', 9 December 2011, http://noticias.univision.com/documentales/la-amenaza-irani/article/2011-12-09/la-amenaza-irani#axzz1hrZoAr4P.

42 'Ray Walser on Iranian Influence in Latin America: Heritage in Focus Podcast', Heritage Foundation, recorded on 13 December 2011, http://www.heritage.org/multimedia/audio/2011/12/walser-podcast-12-13-11.

43 Samuel Rubenfeld, 'FATF Lauds Argentina Anti-Terror Financing Efforts, Seeks More Progress', *Wall Street Journal*, 17 February 2012.

44 'Farc Kills 11 Colombian Soldiers', *Irish Times*, 18 March 2012, http://www.irishtimes.com/newspaper/breaking/2012/0318/breaking43.html.

45 See Elyssa Pachico, 'Panama FARC Camps Highlight Need for Joint Security Work with Colombia', InSight Crime, 29 March 2012, http://insightcrime.org/insight-latest-news/item/2416-panama-farc-camps-highlight-need-for-joint-security-work-with-colombia; Marcella, *War Without Borders*; Nelza Oliveira, 'FARC Trafficking Drugs in Brazil, Officials

Say', 7 June 2010, Infosurhoy.com, http://infosurhoy.com/cocoon/saii/xhtml/en_GB/features/saii/features/main/2010/06/07/feature-02.

46 Mark Burgess, 'Globalizing Terrorism: The FARC–IRA Connection', *Center for Defense Information*, 5 June 2002, http://www.cdi.org/terrorism/farc-ira.cfm.

47 Simon Romero, 'Leaders of Venezuela and Colombia, Ideological Opposites, Are Tightening Ties', *New York Times* 19 October 2007, p. 13.

48 Larry Birns and Jessica Bryant, 'Chávez's Blockbuster Proposal: Finally the Right Message for Peace', Council on Hemispheric Affairs, 10 June 2008, http://www.coha.org/chavez_E2_80_99s-blockbuster-proposal-finally-the-right-message-for-peace/.

49 Romero, 'Leaders of Venezuela and Colombia, Ideological Opposites, Are Tightening Ties'.

50 'Peru – Sendero Luminoso attacks military base', *Latin News Daily Report*, 22 November 2011, http://latinnews.com/component/k2/item/49267.html?period=2011&archive=2&cat_id=786633_3Aperu-E2_80_93-sendero-luminoso-attacks-military-base; 'Artemio' reconoció que Sendero Luminoso fue derrotado', El Comercio.pe, 6 December 2011; Elyssa Pachico, 'Military Statistics Suggest Shining Path Growing in Numbers', InSightCrime.org, 23 December 2011, http://insightcrime.org/component/k2/item/2013-military-statistics-suggest-shining-path-growing-in-numbers.

51 Anagha Krishnan, 'García's Decline in Peru', Council on Hemispheric Affairs, 21 July 2009.

52 See Douglas Chalmers et. al., *The New Politics of Inequality in Latin America: Rethinking Participation and Representation* (New York: Oxford University Press, 1997); Mauricio Cárdenas, 'Political Polarization in Latin America', Brookings Up Front Blog, 6 November 2009, http://www.brookings.edu/opinions/2009/1106_politics_latin_america_cardenas.aspx .

53 See Diego Cevallos, 'Not Everyone Celebrates Improved Poverty Statistics', 23 August 2005, Inter Press Service, http://www.globalpolicy.org/component/content/article/211/45123.html; Barbara J. Fraser, 'Experts: As Economy Grows, Income Disparity in', *Catholic News Service*, 30 July 2007, http://www.globalpolicy.org/component/content/article/218/46559.html.

54 Mark Schuller, 'Haitian Food Riots Unnerving but Not Surprising', 25 April 2008, Americas Program, Center for International Policy, available at http://www.americas.irc-online.org.

55 Though many analysts claim this high degree of inequality goes back to colonial times, a new paper disputes that and dates it from the late nineteenth century. Jeffrey G. Williamson, 'History without Evidence: Latin American Inequality since 1491', NBER Working Paper no. 14766, March 2009.

56 Florencia Torche and Seymour Spilerman, 'Household Wealth in Latin America', Research Paper no. 2006/114 UNU-WIDER, October 2006, pp. 1, 14–15, 35.

57 Ricardo Paes de Barros, Francisco H. G. Ferreira, José R. Molinas Vega and Jaime Saavedra Chanduvi, *Measuring Inequality of Opportunities in Latin America and the Caribbean* (Washington DC: The World Bank, 2008), pp. 1, xviii.

58 'A Slow Maturing of Democracy', *Economist*, 10 December 2009.

59 Chris Kraul, 'Interview with Teodoro Petkoff: A Sort of Centrist Weighs in on Chávez Victory', *Los Angeles Times*, 17 February 2009.

60 See Hannah Stone, 'The Many Political Faces of Daniel Ortega', Council on Hemispheric Affairs, 21 December 2011, http://www.coha.org/the-many-political-faces-of-daniel-ortega/.

61 Unless otherwise noted, data in this section are taken from *Crime, Violence, and Development: Trends, Costs, and Policy Options in the Caribbean*, report no. 37,820, A Joint Report by the United Nations Office on Drugs and Crime and the Latin America and the Caribbean Region of the World Bank, March 2007.

62 Lucia Dammert, *Reporte del Sector Seguridad en América Latina y el Caribe* (Santiago: FLACSO-Chile, 2007), pp. 79–80.

63 See *Ibid.*

64 See 'Online analysis', *Latinobarómetro* 2009, http://www.latinobarometro.org/latino/LATAnalizeIndex.jsp.

65 *Crime, Violence, and Development: Trends, Costs, and Policy Options in the Caribbean*, p. iv.

66 Louisa Reynolds, 'Panama: Drug-Fueled Violence on the Increase', NotiCen, 28 January 2010. The origin of the youth-gang problem dates to 2000–04, when the United States deported about 20,000 young Central American criminals whose families had fled the civil wars in the 1980s and settled in the US. These youths were deported to countries that they barely knew, and US immigration rules at the time banned officials from disclosing the criminal backgrounds of the deportees to receiving-country officials. The *maras* have flourished as the area's youth populations have exploded in the context of great poverty and high unemployment. The *maras* commit thousands of murders and participate in a flourishing drug trade as well as extortion, kidnapping, robbery, international car theft rings, and sophisticated people-smuggling operations. In Tapachula, a Mexican city on the Guatemalan border, the *maras* began maiming and killing undocumented workers heading to Mexico. This was intended as a warning that only those who paid for gang-connected 'coyotes' to smuggle them into the US (at $5,000–8,000 per person) would make it alive. Sam Logan, 'Illegal Migration, Crime and Mexico's Maras', 13 November 2006, mexidata.info.

67 *Latinobarómetro* 2009, pp. 33–4.

68 Amnesty International, 'State of the World's Human Rights: Paraguay', 2011, http://www.amnesty.org/en/region/paraguay/report-2011.

69 .International Crisis Group, 'Colombia: President Uribe's Democratic Security Policy', Latin America Report, no. 6, 13 November 2003, http://www.crisisgroup.org/home/index.cfm?id=2367&l=1; Embassy of Colombia, 'The Uribe Administration's Democratic Security and Defense Policy', Washington DC, http://www.presidencia.gov.co/sne/visita_bush/documentos/security.pdf; Human Rights Watch, 'Colombia: Obama Should Press Uribe on Rights Ahead of Meeting, Concerns Over Record on Democracy, Rule of Law', 26 June 2009.

70 Joseph Vavrus, 'CPJ Report: Journalists Killed with Impunity in Colombia, Mexico, and Brazil', Journalism in the Americas Blog, 2 June 2011, http://knightcenter.utexas.edu/blog/cpj-report-journalists-killed-impunity-colombia-mexico-and-brazil.

Chapter Two

1   See Mares, *Violent Peace.*

2   Jorge Martín, 'The Handing over of Pérez Becerra and the Strategy of the Venezuelan Revolution', 5 May 2011, venezuelanalysis.com, http://venezuelanalysis.com/analysis/6168.

3   David Scott Palmer, 'Peru–Ecuador Border Conflict Missed Opportunities, Misplaced Nationalism, and Multilateral Peacekeeping', *Journal of InterAmerican Studies and World Affairs,* vol. 39, no. 3, autumn 1997, pp. 109–48.

4   Alex Sanchez, 'Bolivia's Military: It's a Difficult Life, but Certainly There Is No Sign of a Pending Military Coup', Council on Hemispheric Affairs, 5 November 2008, http://www.coha.org/bolivia_E280_99s-militaryit_E2_80_99s-a-difficult-life-but-no-sign-of-a-military-coup-yet/.

5   'ALBA Tells OAS to Stay Out of Venezuela's Affairs', *Caribbean Net News,* 22 February 2011, http://www.caribbeannewsnow.com/venezuela.php?news_id=5151&start=0&category_id=12.

6   David A. Baldwin, *Economic Statecraft* (Princeton, NJ: Princeton University Press, 1985); I.M. Destler and John Odell, assisted by Kimberly Ann Elliott, *Anti-Protection: Changing Forces in United States Trade Politics* (Washington DC: Institute for International Economics, 1987); Lisa L. Martin, *Coercive Cooperation: Exploring Multilateral Economic Sanctions* (Princeton, NJ: Princeton University Press, 1992).

7   'Guyana Recommits to Peaceful Resolution of Border Issue with Venezuela', *Caribbean Net News,* 10 July 2010, http://www.caribbeannewsnow.com/caribnet/venezuela/venezuela.php?news_id=23915&start=0&category_id=12; 'Caribbean Leaders Welcome Move to Settle Border Dispute between Guyana and Venezuela', *Caribbean Net News,* 5 March 2011, http://www.caribbeannewsnow.com/venezuela.php?news_id=5345&start=0&category_id=12.

8   Alex Sanchez, 'All is Not Well in Georgetown: Guyana's Emerging Hemispheric Role', Council on Hemispheric Affairs, 23 January 2008, http://www.coha.org/although-all-is-not-well-in-georgetown-guyana_E2_80_99s-emerging-hemispheric-role/.

9   Inter-American Development Bank, 'High Taxes and Evasion Eroding Economic Growth in Latin America and the Caribbean', 4 March 2010, http://www.iadb.org/en/news/webstories/2010-03-04/tax-burden-and-evasion-in-latin-america-idb-study.6619.html.

10 John Baffes, 'Placing the 2006/08 Commodity Price Boom into Perspective', World Bank Blog 'Prospects for Development', 26 July 2010, http://blogs.worldbank.org/prospects/placing-the-200608-commodity-price-boom-into-perspective; 'Commodity Markets' The World Bank, available at http://econ.worldbank.org.

11 'Costa Rica Sends New Police Unit to Border', TicoTimes.net, 31 March 2011, http://www.ticotimes.net/Current-Edition/News-Briefs/Costa-Rica-sends-new-police-unit-to-border_Thursday-March-31-2011.

12 Mares, *Violent Peace*, pp. 132–55.

13 'La Renovación es Justificada, pero la Cantidad Adquirida No', *Correo,*

1 November 2009, reproduced in *Enfoque Estratégico*, 9 November 2009, http://www.enfoque-estrategico.com/reportajes/cesar_cruz.htm.

14 Mike Ceaser, 'Chávez's "Citizen Militias" on the March', BBC, 1 July 2005; Kiraz Janicke, 'Venezuela Creates Peasant Militias, Enacts Federal Government Council', Venezuelanalysis.com, 22 February 2010, http://venezuelanalysis.com/news/5150.

15 'Colombia y Brasil Negocian Plan Binacional de Seguridad Fronteriza', 2 July 2011, http://maquina-de-combate.com/blog/archives/16566.

16 '11 April 2011: World military spending reached $1.6 trillion in 2010, biggest increase in South America, fall in Europe according to new SIPRI data', http://www.sipri.org/media/pressreleases/milex.

17 '15 Mar 2010: New SIPRI data on international arms transfers reflect arms race concerns', http://www.sipri.org/media/pressreleases/2010/100315armstransfers.

18 'Arms-R-Us: South America Goes Shopping: A WOLA Report on South American Defense Expenditures', March 2010, http://www.seguridadfip.org/boletinestudiosdefensa/boletin4oestudios/ArmsRUsSouthAmericaGoesShopping.pdf.

19 Chile's submarines have significantly better technology than Peru's, giving Chile advantages in days at sea, detection of targets and combat capabilities. 'La Renovación es Justificada, pero la Cantidad Adquirida No'.

20 *The Military Balance 2011* (London: Routledge for IISS), pp. 352–3.

21 James Brooke, 'Fiery Nationalism Drove Venezuelan Plotters', *New York Times*, 11 February 1992, p. A6.

22 Venezuelan military posturing is not new. In 1979, Venezuelan planes overflew Costa Rica as a warning to the Somoza government about pursuing rebels into Costa Rican territory.

23 Alfred Stepan, *Military in Politics: Changing Patterns in Brazil* (Princeton, NJ: Princeton University Press, 1971); Luigi R. Einaudi, *The Peruvian Military* (Santa Monica, CA: RAND, 1969).

24 John Sweeney, 'Venezuela and Colombia: The FAN is Outmatched' Hispanic American Center for Economic Research, 2006, http://www.hacer.org/current/Vene035.php.

25 Sara Miller Llana, 'Venezuela's Chávez Softens Stance', *Christian Science Monitor*, 14 July 2008.

26 Stephen J. Blank, 'Russia and Latin America: Motives and Consequences', Center for Hemispheric Policy, University of Miami, 13 April 2010, p. 10.

27 R. Evan Ellis, *China–Latin America Military Engagement: Good Will, Good Business, and Strategic Position* (Carlyle, PA: Strategic Studies Institute, US Army War College, 2011).

28 Latin American Data Base, 'Nicaraguan Missiles and Honduran Warplanes on Political Collision Course', *NotiCen*, 2 August 2007.

29 Susan Abad, 'Fábricas de armas y municiones de Venezuela desequilibrarían la región', *El Comercio*, Peru, www.elcomercioperu.com.pe?EdicionImpresa/Html/2006-12-17/ImEcMundo0634393.html; Matthew Walter, 'Chávez Goes Weapons Shopping in Russia Amid Arms Race (Update2)', Bloomberg.com, 21 July 2008.

30 'Supplemental Agreement for Cooperation and Technical Assistance

in Defense and Security between the governments of The United States of America and the Republic of Colombia, 11 November 2009', cited in 'Arms R Us'.

31 Nathaniel Frandino, 'Chile to Send Army to Guard Bolivian Border', *Santiago Times*, 13 July 2011, http://santiagotimes.cl/atacama-times/regional-news/21960-chile-to-send-army-to-guard-bolivian-border.

32 J.C. Arancibia, 'Bolivian Troops Cross Into Chile', *Chile's Defense and Military*, 17 June 2011, http://chiledefense.blogspot.com/2011/06/bolivian-troops-cross-into-chile.html.

33 'Autoridades de ambos países coincidirán en Mercosur y luego en CELAC: Chile y Bolivia se reencuentran en citas cumbres tras tensas semanas', *El Mercurio*, 27 June 2011, http://diario.elmercurio.com/detalle/index.asp?id={32f7156b-a74e-4cd5-a721-3e6c3beb5d1a}.

34 The combination of nationalism and populism can come together across a wide spectrum of political ideologies, from left to right; hence the concept of national populism doesn't necessarily imply fascist-style, right-wing nationalist movements. See Yannis Papadopoulos, 'National-Populism in Western Europe: An Ambivalent Phenomenon', unpublished MS, Institut d'Etudes Politiques et Internationales, Université de Lausanne; see also, Kurt Weyland, 'Clarifying a Contested Concept: Populism in the Study of Latin American Politics', *Comparative Politics*, vol. 34, no. 1, October 2001, pp. 1–22.

35 John Daly, 'Bolivia's Natural Gas Reserves Now on Political Firing Line', OilPrice.com, 7 March 2012, http://oilprice.com/Energy/Natural-Gas/Bolivias-Natural-Gas-Reserves-Now-on-Political-Firing-Line.htm.

36 'Bolivia: Investment Dries Up', *Petroleum Economist*, July 2008 http://www.petroleum-economist.com/default.asp?page=14&PubID=46&ISS=24836&SID=708318.

37 See Richard K. Betts, *Soldiers, Statesmen and Cold War Crises* (Cambridge, MA: Harvard University Press, 1977).

Chapter Three

1 Jeremy McDermott, 'Colombia Border Province Sees Rebel Attacks Increase', BBC News, 18 June 2011, http://www.bbc.co.uk/news/world-latin-america-13762982.

2 Alberto Rovira, 'Colombia's Santos Not Interested in Peace Talks with FARC', Infosurhoy.com, 14 February 2011, http://www.infosurhoy.com/cocoon/saii/xhtml/en_GB/features/saii/features/main/2011/02/14/feature-03.

3 Adriaan Alsema, 'Santos' Urban Approval Rating at 67%: Gallup', Colombiareports.com, 1 July 2011, http://colombiareports.com/colombia-news/news/17333-santos-urban-approval-rating-at-67-gallup.html; Arturo Wallace, 'Colombia's FARC Rebels: Retreating or Resurgent?', BBC News, 19 July 2011, http://www.bbc.co.uk/news/world-latin-america-14186159.

4   'Colombia's Santos Outlines New Tactics against Rebels', BBC News, 8 August 2011, http://www.bbc.co.uk/news/world-latin-america-14441241.

5   'Colombia Defence Minister Resigns; Deep Reshuffle in Forces Anticipated', MercoPress, 31 August 2011, http://en.mercopress.com/2011/08/31/colombia-defence-minister-resigns-deep-reshuffle-in-forces-anticipated.

6   César Morales Colón, 'Colombia Security Force Score with "Operation Sword of Honor"', Infosurhoy.com, 22 March 2012, http://infosurhoy.com/cocoon/saii/xhtml/en_GB/features/saii/features/main/2012/03/22/feature-03.

7   Jack Kimball, 'Colombia Rebel Hit Doesn't Boost Santos Popularity', Reuters, 16 November 2011, http://www.trust.org/alertnet/news/colombia-rebel-hit-doesnt-boost-santos-popularity.

8   Milburn Line, 'Trying to End Colombia's Battle with FARC', Foreign Affairs, 27 March 2012, http://www.foreignaffairs.com/articles/137354/milburn-line/trying-to-end-colombias-battle-with-farc?page=2.

9   US Government Accounting Office, 'Drug Reduction Goals Were Not Fully Met, but Security Has Improved; US Agencies Need More Detailed Plans for Reducing Assistance', GAO-09-71, 6 October 2008.

10   Jeremy McDermott 'Colombia's Rebels: A Fading Force?', BBC News, 1 February 2008, http://news.bbc.co.uk/2/hi/americas/7217817.stm; Frank Bajak, 'Colombia's FARC Executes 4 Captives', Associated Press, 26 November 2011, http://www.huffingtonpost.com/2011/11/26/colombias-farc-executions_n_1114624.html.

11   The Military Balance 2012 (London, Routledge for IISS), pp. 364 and 404. Inflation hit 28.2% in 2010, and dropped only slightly to 25.8% in 2011.

12   'ARMY, Venezuela', Jane's Sentinel Security Assessment – South America, 13 November 2007, http://www.janes.com/articles/indepth/sams.html.

13   'ARMY, Colombia', Jane's Sentinel Security Assessment – South America, 14 February 2008, http://www.janes.com/articles/indepth/sams.html.

14   'Colombian Exports to Venezuela Are Vital', El Universal, 28 July 2009, http://english.eluniversal.com/2009/07/28/en_eco_esp_colombian-exports-to_28A2552123.shtml.

15   Drew Benson and Matthew Walter, 'Colombia Peso Drops Most in a Month as Venezuela Blocks Imports', Bloomberg.com, 29 July 2009.

16   Alan Fairlie Reinoso, 'Peru and Colombia: Similar Strategies, Contrasting Reactions', Latin America Trade Network, August 2010, http://www.latn.org.ar/web/wp-content/uploads/2011/03/FLA_GTA_06_Peru-Col_Septo6.pdf; Elyssa Pachico ,'Venezuelan Trade Ban Hurts Colombia', Colombiareports.com, 24 February 2010, http://colombiareports.com/colombia-news/economy/8392-venezuelan-trade-ban-hurting-colombia-study-finds.html.

17   IISS, The FARC Files.

18   Colombia did not mobilise additional forces to the borders after Chávez ordered the deployment of 9,000 soldiers, tanks and planes and Ecuador deployed 3,200 troops to the regions. Patrick Goodenough, 'US, Colombia Call for Calm Over Military Incursion Clash', CNSNews.com, 3 March 2008; Peter Walker, 'Ecuador Ready for "Ultimate Consequences" in Regional Crisis', Guardian, 5 March 2008, http://www.guardian.

co.uk/world/2008/mar/04/colombia. venezuela.

19 Brian Ellsworth, 'Venezuela Mobilizes Forces to Colombia Border', Reuters, 5 March 2008, http://www.reuters.com/article/topNews/idUSN0227633020080 305?feedType=RSS&feedName=topN ews.

20 'Colombians Would Vote Again for Uribe', Angus Reid Global Monitor: Polls & Research, 29 March 2008, http://www.angus-reid.com/polls/view/colombians_would_vote_again_ for_uribe/.

21 'Uribe Right About Venezuela, Say Colombians', Angus Reid Global Monitor: Polls & Research, 29 January 2008, http://www.angus-reid.com/polls/view/uribe_right_about_ venezuela_say_colombians/.

22 Alsema, 'Santos' Urban Approval Rating at 67%: Gallup'.

23 Angus Reid Global Monitor: Polls & Research, 'Colombia, Ecuador Assess Cross-border Incursion', poll conducted by Centro Nacional de Consultoría and Cedatos-Gallup, released by C&M, 9 March 2008, http://www.angus-reid.com/polls/view/30098/colombia_ecuador_assess_ cross_border_incursion.

24 'Venezuelans Don't Want War with Colombia', Angus Reid Global Monitor: Polls & Research, 14 March 2008, http://www.angus-reid.com/polls/view/venezuelans_dont_want_ war_with_colombia/.

25 This was part of his rhetoric when he rushed in to the Colombia–Ecuador dispute. Ellsworth, 'Venezuela Mobilizes Forces to Colombia Border'.

26 Martín, 'The Handing Over of Pérez Becerra'.

27 See Reporters without Borders, 'Colombia', http://en.rsf.org/colombia.

html; Liam Whittington, 'A Legal Wasteland – Lawyers, Murder, Democracy, and Justice in Colombia', Council on Hemispheric Affairs, 4 December 2011, http://www.coha.org/a-legal-wasteland-E28093-lawyers-murder-democracy-and-justice-in-colombia/.

28 'Democracy and Human Rights in Venezuela', Inter-American Commission on Human Rights, OAS, OEA/Ser.L/V/II, 30 December 2009, http://cidh.org/countryrep/Venezuela2009eng/VE09.TOC.eng.htm.

29 David Blair, 'Chávez Running Out of Time as Allies Desert him', Daily Telegraph, 30 June 2008.

30 Tamara Pearson, 'Venezuelan President Says OAS General Secretary Distorts Army Head's Words on 2012 Elections', 12 November 2010, http://venezuelanalysis.com/news/5781; Daniel Cancel, 'Chavez Promotes Venezuela General Criticized for Threat Against Opposition', 11 November 2010, Bloomberg, http://www.bloomberg.com/news/2010-11-12/chavez-promotes-venezuela-general-criticized-for-threat-against-opposition.html.

31 'The Bolivarian Patient', Economist, 7 July 2011, www.economist.com/node/18928536.

32 Clare Ribando Seelke, 'Ecuador: Political and Economic Situation and US Relations', Congressional Research Service, Order Code RS21687, updated 21 May 2008; Arthur Brice, 'Arrest Warrant Derails Colombia–Ecuador Talks', CNN.com, 17 October 2009.

33 Adriaan Alsema, 'Colombia Thanks Ecuador for Military Assistance, Ecuador Denies Help', Colombia Reports, 20 September 2010, http://

colombiareports.com/colombia-news/
news/11930-colombia-thanks-ecuador-
for-military-assistance-ecuador-
denies-help.html.

34 Pablo Celi, 'Ecuador: Redefiniciones
Políticas, Ajustes Institucionales y
Proyección Regional', *Atlas Comparativo
de la Defensa en América Latina 2010*
(Buenos Aires: RESDAL, 2010), p.
200; 'Colombia/Ecuador Re-establish
Trade Relations After 21 Months',
MercoPress, 25 November 2009,
http://en.mercopress.com/2009/11/24/
colombia-ecuador-re-establish-trade-
relations-after-21-months.

35 IISS, *The FARC Files.*

36 'ARMY, Ecuador', *Jane's Sentinel
Security Assessment – South America*,
30 November 2007, http://www.janes.
com/articles/indepth/sams.html.

37 Figures are in US dollars. *The Military
Balance 2011* (London: Routledge for
the IISS, 2011), p. 371.

38 Celi, 'Ecuador: Redefiniciones
Políticas', p. 201.

39 See *The Military Balance 2011*, pp. 353–4,
366–8, 371–3; and *The Military Balance
2012*, pp. 381–4 and 387–9.

40 'Colombia, Ecuador Drop Plans to
Restore Diplomatic Ties', AFP, 24 June
2008, http://afp.google.com/article/
ALeqM5guoiEMNxBwKOHu4QW_
dCQArUaAnA .

41 Brice, 'Arrest Warrant Derails
Colombia–Ecuador Talks'.

42 'Colombia's Borders: The Weak Link
In Uribe's Security Policy', *Latin
America Report*, no. 9, Quito and
Brussels: International Crisis Group,
23 September 2004.

43 Marcella, *War Without Borders*; IISS, *The
FARC Files*.

44 Marcella, *War Without Borders*, p. 5.

45 'Steady Numbers for President Correa
in Ecuador', Angus Reid Global

Monitor: Polls & Research, 27 February 2008, http://www.angus-reid.com/
polls/view/steady_numbers_for_pres-
ident_correa_in_ecuador/; 'Ecuador
Disappointed with Constituent Assembly', Angus Reid Global Monitor:
Polls & Research, 20 February 2008,
http://www.angus-reid.com/polls/
view/ecuador_disappointed_with_
constituent_assembly/.

46 Marcella, *War Without Borders*, p. 33.

47 'Cheetahs and Mirage 50s for
Ecuador', *Defense Industry Daily*,
14 December 2010, http://www.
defenseindustrydaily.com/Cheetahs-
and-Mirage-50s-for-Ecudaor-05832/;
http://www.flightglobal.com/news/
articles/ecuador-looks-to-trim-super-
tucano-purchase-342724/; *The Military
Balance 2012*, p. 387.

48 'ICJ Rules on Costa Rica–Nicaragua
River Dispute', International Boundary
Research Unit, Durham University, 13
July 2009, available at http://www.
dur.ac.uk/ibru/resources/newsarchive/
search_results/.

49 Nicky Pear and Alexandra Reed,
'Dredging Up an Old Issue: An
Analysis of the Long-Standing Dispute
between Costa Rica and Nicaragua
over the San Juan River', Council on
Hemispheric Affairs, 24 January 2011,
http://www.coha.org/dredging-up-
an-old-issue-an-analysis-of-the-long-
standing-dispute-between-costa-rica-
and-nicaragua-over-the-san-juan-
river-2/.

50 Isla Celros itself is undisputed Costa
Rican territory.

51 Confidential interviews with Costa
Rican scholars at FLACSO General
Secretariat, San Jose, Costa Rica, 11
April 2011.

52 'Troop Pull-Out Urged In Nicaragua–
Costa Rica Border Row', BBC

News, 14 November 2010, http://www.bbc.co.uk/news/world-latin-america-11751727; Pear and Reed, 'Dredging Up an Old Issue'; Alex Sanchez, 'Costa Rica: An Army-less Nation in a Problem-Prone Region', Council on Hemispheric Affairs, 2 June 2011, http://www.coha.org/costa-rica-an-army-less-nation-in-a-problem-prone-region/; 'Costa Rica Bets On Stiffer Border Security As It Waits For ICJ Measures To Start Normalizing', NotiCen, Central American & Caribbean Affairs, Latin American Database, 7 April 2011.

53 Confidential interviews with Costa Rican scholars at FLACSO General Secretariat, 11 April 2011, San Jose, Costa Rica

54 *Ibid.*

55 Marianela Jimenez, 'Costa Rica Denounces Alleged Nicaraguan Incursion', Associated Press, 2 November 2010, http://www.washingtonpost.com/wp-dyn/content/article/2010/11/02/AR2010110203621.html.

56 *Ibid.*

57 Esteban Oviedo, 'Canciller Dice Que Managua Permite A Civiles Violar La Zona Restringida', *El Pais*, 25 June 2011, http://www.nacion.com/2011-06-25/ElPais/pais-denuncia--a-nicaragua-por-alentar-incursiones-a-isla-calero.aspx.

58 Michael Brecher and Jonathan Wilkenfeld, *A study of crisis* (Ann Arbor, MI: University of Michigan Press, 1997) pp. 134–5.

59 'Costa Rica', Camopaedia.org, http://camopedia.org/index.php?title=Costa_Rica.

60 *The Military Balance 2011*, p. 368.

61 'Debutó la Policía de Fronteras de Costa Rica', infobae.com, 31 March 2011, http://america.infobae.com/notas/22029-La-Policia-de-Fronteras-de-Costa-Rica-debuto-con-la-movilizacion-de-153-agentes.

62 *A Comparative Atlas of Defence in Latin America and the Caribbean 2010*, chapter 22, 'Nicaragua', RESDAL, pp. 255, 259, http://www.resdal.org/atlas/atlas10-ing-22-nicaragua.pdf; *The Military Balance 2012*, p. 397.

63 *Military Balance 2011*, p. 381.

64 Pear and Read, 'Dredging Up an Old Issue'.

65 Dovelyn Agunias, 'Remittance Trends in Central America', Migration Information Source, April 2006, http://www.migrationinformation.org/USfocus/display.cfm?ID=393.

66 Ricardo Monge-González, Oswald Céspedes-Torres and Juan Carlos Vargas-Aguilar, *South–South Remittances: Importance of the Costa Rica–Nicaragua Corridor* (San Jose: Academia de Centroamérica, 2009) pp, 5–7, 21.

67 Pear and Read, 'Dredging Up an Old Issue'.

68 Department of State, 'Background Note: Nicaragua', http://www.state.gov/r/pa/ei/bgn/1850.htm; Gisella Canales Ewest, 'Ticos Buscan Vender Mas en Nicaragua', *La Prensa.com.ni*, 1 July 2010, http://www.laprensa.com.ni/2010/07/01/economia/29868#.Tk6jpF1vDrc.

69 Sanchez, 'Costa Rica: An Army-less Nation in a Problem-Prone Region'.

70 Sanchez, 'Costa Rica'; 'Debutó la Policía', infobae.com; 'Costa Rica Sends New Police Unit to Border', TicoTimes, 31 March 2011, http://www.ticotimes.net/Current-Edition/News-Briefs/Costa-Rica-sends-new-police-unit-to-border_Thursday-March-31-2011.

71 Sanchez, 'Costa Rica'.

72 Carlos Arroyo Borgen, 'From Guerrilla to Institutional Consolidation: the Special Evolution of the Nicaraguan Army', in *A Comparative Atlas of Defence in Latin America and the Caribbean 2010*, RESDAL, p. 263, citing M&R Consultores, 'Nicaragua, Sistema de Monitoreo de la Opinión Pública (SISMO) Edición XXV Junio 2010', http://www.myrconsultores.com/page/estudios.html.

73 Pear and Read, 'Dredging Up an Old Issue'.

74 'Blunders Force Tijerino From Seguridad', Insidecostarica.com, 26 April 2011, http://www.insidecostarica.com/dailynews/2011/april/26/costarica11042501.htm.

75 Pear and Read, 'Dredging Up an Old Issue'.

76 For an insightful discussion of Ortega, see Hannah Stone, 'The Many Political Faces of Daniel Ortega', Council on Hemispheric Affairs, 21 December 2011, http://www.coha.org/the-many-political-faces-of-daniel-ortega/.

77 'Arranca Nueva Legislatura en Costa Rica', TodaNoticia.com, 1 May 2010 http://www.todanoticia.com/12089/arranca-nueva-legislatura-costa-rica/.

78 Peter Amsel, 'Costa Rica Shelves Tax Plan for Land-based Casino and Online Gaming Operators', CalvinAyre.com, 30 March 2011, http://calvinayre.com/2011/03/30/business/costa-rica-shelves-gambling-tax-plan/.

79 In 1976–77 Peru mobilised its military forces to the border to dissuade an apparent deal between Chile and Bolivia, in which a territorial exchange would be made to cede former Peruvian territory to Bolivia in exchange for Bolivian territory in the south. The deal collapsed, but only as a result of the fear of war breaking out if it were consummated.

80 República del Bolivia, Constitución de 2009, Article 267, http://pdba.georgetown.edu/Constitutions/Bolivia/bolivia09.html; Karin Ebensperger, 'Bolivia otra vez', *El Mercurio*, 5 April 2011, available via Universidad Andrés Bello, http://blog.unab.cl/defensa/2011/04/06/bolivia-otra-vez-columna-de-karin-ebensperger-el-mercurio-5-de-abril-de-2011/.

81 Julie McCarthy, 'Bachelet Takes Oath as Chile's President', National Public Radio, 11 March 2006.

82 'Autoridades de ambos países coincidirán en Mercosur y luego en CELAC: Chile y Bolivia se reencuentran en citas cumbres tras tensas semanas', *El Mercurio*, 27 June 2011, http://diario.elmercurio.com/detalle/index.asp?id={32f7156b-a74e-4cd5-a721-3e6c3beb5d1a}.

83 Jeanna Cullinan, 'Chile Plans to Crack Down on Trafficking Over Bolivia Border', *InSight*, 5 October 2011, http://www.insightcrime.org/insight-latest-news/item/1660-chile-plans-to-crack-down-on-trafficking-over-bolivia-border.

84 Rick DelVecchio, 'Haitian Migrants Face Violence in the Dominican Republic', *Catholic San Francisco*, 4 December 2009.

85 *Latinobarómetro 2010*, p. 36.

86 'Half of Argentines Believe Malvinas Conflict "Will Never Be Solved", Shows Poll', MercoPress, 4 April 2012.

87 'Mrs. Kirchner Calls UN to Force UK to Falklands' Sovereignty Negotiations', MercoPress.com, 17 February 2010, http://en.mercopress.com/2010/02/17/mrs.-kirchner-calls-un-to-force-uk-to-falklands-sovereignty-negotiations;

'Argentine Protests Falklands Oil Drilling before the Rio Group and UN', MercoPress.com, 18 February 2010, http://en.mercopress.com/2010/02/18/argentine-protests-falklands-oil-drilling-before-the-rio-group-and-un.

88 'Argentine Protests Falklands Oil Drilling before the Rio Group and UN'.

89 'Cristina Fernandez Abandons Summit with No Declaration on Falklands/Malvinas', MercoPress, 15 April 2012.

90 'UK Committed to Falklands in Spite of all the "Huff and Puff" from Argentine Politicians'.

91 The Argentine Constitution of 1994 stipulates that the Malvinas, South Georgia and South Sandwich Islands are national territory and will be regained according to the principles of international law. See Political Database of the Americas, http://pdba.georgetown.edu/Constitutions/Argentina/argen94_e.html.

Chapter Four

1 'Plan Colombia', Insightcrime.org, http://insightcrime.org/security-police/plan-colombia/item/5-plan-colombia.

2 Clare Ribando Seelke and Kristin M. Finklea, U.S.–Mexican Security Cooperation: The Mérida Initiative and Beyond (Washington DC: Congressional Research Service, 15 August 2011).

3 Latin American Commission on Drugs and Democracy, Drugs and Democracy: Towards a Paradigm Shift, 2009, http://www.drogasedemocracia.org/English/.

4 Dave Graham, 'Mexico President Hints Legalizing Drugs May Be Needed', Reuters, 20 September 2011, http://af.reuters.com/article/worldNews/idAFTRE78J0KL20110920?sp=true.

5 'Biden Visits Honduras Amid Drug Legalization Debate', CNN, 6 March 2012, http://articles.cnn.com/2012-03-06/americas/world_americas_honduras-biden_1_drug-legalization-drug-trafficking-legalization-or-decriminalization?_s=PM:AMERICAS.

6 Susanne Gratius, 'Brazil in the Americas: A Regional Peace Broker?', Working Paper no. 35 (Madrid: Fundación para las Relaciones Internacionales y el Diálogo Exterior (FRIDE, April 2007), p. 27; Cynthia J. Arnson and Paulo Sotero, 'Brazil as a Regional Power: Views from the Hemisphere', Latin America Program, Woodrow Wilson International Center for Scholars, 2010, pp. 13–4, http://www.wilsoncenter.org/sites/default/files/WWC_Brazil-Institute-Report-updated%200926101.pdf.

7 'Brazil's Economy Overtakes UK to Become World's Sixth Largest', Guardian, 6 March 2012, www.guardian.co.uk/business/.../brazil-economy-worlds-sixth-largest.

8 CIA World Factbook, https://www.cia.gov/library/publications/the-world-factbook/geos/br.html.

9 Nathan Gill, 'Ecuador, Odebrecht in Talks Over Asset Seizure, May Reach Accord Next Week', 21 May 2010, http://www.bloomberg.com/news/2010-05-21/ecuador-odebrecht-in-talks-over-asset-seizure-may-reach-accord-next-week.html.

10 'Falklands Vessels Can Re-flag and Operate in Mercosur Ports, Says Hague', MercoPress, 20 January 2012.

11 Rebecca Gorn, 'Brazil's Real(ly) Big Problem', Council on Hemispheric Affairs, 9 September 2011, http://diplomatizzando.blogspot.com/2011/09/council-on-hemispheric-affairs-mercosur.html.

12 'Brazil Breaks Relations With Human Rights Commission Over Belo Monte Dam', Latin American News Dispatch, 3 May 2011, http://latindispatch.com/2011/05/03/brazil-breaks-relations-with-human-rights-commission-over-belo-monte-dam/.

13 Russell Crandall, 'The Post-American Hemisphere, Power and Politics in an Autonomous Latin America', Foreign Affairs, May–June 2011, p. 89.

14 Alex Sanchez, 'Endgame for Brazil's Role in MINUSTAH?', Council on Hemispheric Affairs, 29 August 2011, http://www.coha.org/endgame-for-brazils-role-in-minustah/.

15 Ministry of Defense, National Strategy of Defense 2008, p. 8, www.defesa.gov.br.

16 Ibid., p. 16.

17 Celso Amorim, 'Let Us In: Why Barack Obama Must Support Brazil's Drive For A Permanent Seat On The U.N. Security Council', Foreign Policy, 14 March 2011, http://www.foreignpolicy.com/articles/2011/03/14/let_us_in.

18 Daniel Flemes and Alcides Costa Vaz, 'Security Policies of India, Brazil and South Africa', German Institute of Global and Area Studies, Working Paper no. 160, February 2011, p. 13.

19 'Minister Assures International Projects of Defense And Fighters', Inforel.org, 3 March 2011, http://www.inforel.org/noticias/noticia_Ingles.php?not_id=4728; The Military Balance 2012, pp. 366–9.

20 'Brazil Shoot-down Policy for Unidentified Aircrafts', MercoPress, 18 October 2004.

21 The Military Balance 2012, p. 367; Samantha Pearson, 'Brazil To Spend $6bn on Border Controls – Report', Reuters, 9 January 2011.

22 'Brazil's Porous Jungle Borders', IISS Strategic Comments, 30 August 2011, vol. 17, no. 30, 30 August 2011.

23 Ricardo Bonalume Neto, 'Exercício das Forças Armadas brasileiras em Itaipu preocupa Paraguai', Forças Terrestres, 31 August 2011, http://www.forte.jor.br/2009/11/16/exercicio-das-forcas-armadas-brasileiras-em-itaipu-preocupa-paraguai/.

24 See Flemes and Costa Vaz, 'Security Policies of India, Brazil and South Africa'.

25 Fernando 'Nunão' De Martini, 'Paraguai Tenta Mobilizar MST Contra Planalto', Forças Terrestres, 9 January 2009, http://www.forte.jor.br/2009/01/09/paraguai-tenta-mobilizar-mst-contra-planalto/.

26 Arnson and Sotero, Brazil As a Regional Power, pp. 3–4.

27 Jean Daudelin, 'Expanding the Latin American Reserve Fund: Is UNASUR Taking On the IMF?', 18 August 2011, http://www.jacaremirim.com/2011/08/expanding-latin-american-reserve-fund.html.

28 Michelle Bachelet Jeria, 'Fifth Conference of Ministers of Defense of the Americas: Report of the Outgoing Chair', Committee on Hemispheric Security, OEA/Ser. G. CP/CSH/INF.19/03 add. 1, 25 February 2003, p. 4.

29 Summits of the Americas Secretariat, 'Previous Summits', http://www.

summit-americas.org/previous_summits.html.

30 Department of State, 'American Treaty on Pacific Settlement', http://www.state.gov/p/wha/rls/70580.htm.

31 The Rio Group was created in 1986 out of the Contadora and Contadora Support Group that had been mediating the US and Nicaragua conflict. The group remained active beyond that issue and today includes all the Latin American states. The US and Canada are not members. It has been the incubator for the new Community of Latin American and Caribbean States (CELAC by its Spanish name).

32 OAS, 'Inter-American Democratic Charter', 11 September 2001, http://www.oas.org/charter/docs/resolution1_en_p4.htm; see also Allan R. Brewer-Carías, *Dismantling Democracy in Venezuela: The Chávez Authoritarian Experiment* (New York: Cambridge University Press, 2010)

33 Conference of Defense Ministers of the Americas, http://www.cdmamericas.org/PublicPages/Home.aspx.

34 OAS, 'The OAS Peace Fund', peacefund@oas.org.

35 OAS, 'Signatories and Ratifications: A-64: Inter-American Convention on Transparency in Conventional Weapons Acquisitions', http://www.oas.org/juridico/english/sigs/a-64.html.

36 Permanent Council of the Organization of American States, Committee on Hemispheric Security, 'Compendium of Replies of the Member States to the Questionnaire on New Approaches to Hemispheric Security', OEA/Ser.G CP/CSH-430/02 rev. 1, 1 October 2002, p.34 www.oas.org/csh/english/documents/cp10269e07.doc.

37 José Antonio Sanahuja, 'Multilateralismo y regionalismo en clave suramericana: El caso de UNASUR', *Pensamiento Propio*, vol. 33, January–June 2011, p. 124.

38 Sanahuja, 'Multilateralismo y regionalismo'; Andrés Serbin, 'Regionalismo y Soberanía Nacional en América Latina: los Nuevos Desafíos', *Nueva Sociedad*, vol. 42, May–June 2010, pp. 70–86.

39 'Declaración de Santiago de Chile', March 2009, http://www.flacso.org/uploads/media/Declaracion_de_Santiago_de_Chile.pdf.

40 'Bolivian, Brazilian Ministers Discuss Proposed Defence Council', BBC Monitoring Latin America – Political (text of a report by Bolivian newspaper *La Prensa*, 21 May 2008).

41 'Colombia and Ecuador Work To Restore Diplomatic Relations', InfosurHoy, 1 October 2009, http://www.infosurhoy.com/cocoon/saii/xhtml/en_GB/features/saii/features/2009/09/30/feature-04.

42 Andrés Serbin, 'Multipolaridad, Liderazgos E Instituciones Regionales: Los Desafíos de la UNASUR Ante la Prevención de Crisis Regionales', *Anuario* 2009–2010, CEIPAZ-Fundación Cultura de Paz, Icaria 2009, p. 239, http://www.ceipaz.org/images/contenido/AndresSerbin.pdf.

43 'Unasur Summit In Argentina To Demand Details of Colombia–USA Base Deal', BBC Monitoring Latin America – Political, text of a report by Ecuadoran newspaper *El Universo*, 11 August 2009.

44 Simon Romero, 'Leaders Repair Colombia–Venezuela Ties', *New York Times*, 10 August 2010.

45 John Chipman and James Lockhart Smith, 'South America: Framing

Regional Security', *Survival*, vol. 51, no. 6, December 2009–January 2010, pp. 77–104.

[46] South American Defence Council, 'Declaración de Guayaquil II Reunión Ordinaria CDS', 7 May 2010; and 'III Reunión Ordinaria Del Consejo De Defensa Suramericano: Declaración De Lima', 12–13 May 2011.

[47] 'Unasur Leaders To Debate Venezuela And Colombia Crisis', BBC, 25 July 2010, http://www.bbc.co.uk/news/world-latin-america-10754663.

[48] W. Alex Sanchez, 'Global Insider: UNASUR Defense Agencies Search for Relevance', *World Politics Review*, 8 February 2012; 'Unasur Members Begin Sharing Information on Defence Expenditure', MercoPress, 30 January 2012.

[49] 'UNASUR Agrees to Boost Defense Expenditure Transparency', MercoPress, 10 May 2010.

[50] 'South American Defense Ministers Discuss Regional Security Issues in Lima', NTN24 News.Com, 11 November 2011, http://www.ntn24.com/news/news/south-american-defense-ministers-discuss-regional-security-issues-lima.

[51] For a discussion of press issues, see Committee to Protect Journalists, http://www.cpj.org/americas/2011/; and Roy Greenslade, 'Press Freedom Fears as Ecuador President Rages Against the Media He Doesn't Control', Greenslade Blog, 9 November 2011, http://www.guardian.co.uk/media/greenslade/2011/nov/09/press-freedom-ecuador.

[52] Central American Integration System, http://www.sica.int/sica/sica_breve_en.aspx?IdEnt=401&Idm=2&IdmStyle=2.

[53] 'Framework Treaty on Democratic Security in Central America. Concluded at San Pedro Sula on 15 December 1995', United Nations — Treaty Series, 1998, p. 217, http://idw.csfederalismo.it/attachments/242_Framework_Treaty_on_democratic_security_in_Central_America.pdf.

[54] Marcelo Monzón, 'Guatemala: Journalism Under Pressure', Opendemocracy.net, 25 September 2005, http://www.opendemocracy.net/media-journalismwar/guatemala_2865.jsp.

[55] Manuel Orozco, 'Conflictos Fronterizos en América Central: Tendencias Pasadas y Sucesos Actuales', in Jorge Domínguez (ed.), *Conflictos Territoriales y Democracia en América Latina* (Argentina: Siglo Veintiuno, 2003), pp. 144–6.

[56] Josette Altmann Borbón, 'ALBA: From integration alternative to political and ideological Alliance', in Canadian Foundation for the Americas (FOCAL), *Latin American Multilateralism: New Directions* (Ottawa: FOCAL, September 2010), p. 29, http://www.iadb.org/intal/intalcdi/PE/2010/06396.pdf.

Conclusion

1 See Carlos Malamud Rikles, 'El Consejo Suramericano De Defensa: Entre Grandes Expectativas Y Una Realidad Compleja y Fraccionada', in *La Creación de Unasur en el Marco de la Seguridad y la Defensa* (Madrid: Ministerio de Defensa, January 2010), pp. 58–67.
2 Louise Arbour, 'Next Year's Wars: Ten Conflicts to Watch in 2012', *Foreign Policy*, no. 27, December 2011, http://www.foreignpolicy.com/articles/2011/12/27/next_years_wars?page=full.
3 Michael Shifter, 'Latin American Multilateralism: New Directions', in *Latin American Multilateralism: New Directions* (Ottawa: Canadian Foundation for the Americas (FOCAL), 28 September 2010).
4 See Francisco Rojas Aravena, 'The Community of Latin American and Caribbean States: A Viable Option to Consolidate Latin American Multilateralism?', *Latin American Multilateralism*, pp. 18–22.
5 Krista E. Wiegand and Emilia Justynia Powell, 'Unexpected Companions: Bilateral Cooperation between States Involved in Territorial Disputes', *Conflict Management and Peace Studies*, vol. 28, 2011, p. 209.
6 Beth Simmons, 'Trade and Territorial Conflict in Latin America: International Borders as Institutions', in Miles Kahler and Barbara F. Walter (eds), *Territoriality and Conflict in an Era of Globalization* (Cambridge: Cambridge University Press, 2006), p. 266. Simmons calculated the average annual loss in bilateral trade at $35 million and calls it significant. But when considering its significance, what should matter is the impact of the loss, not its specific amount. In 1995, Ecuador's GDP was $18 billion, while Peru's was $59bn, dwarfing the lost bilateral trade (see International Monetary Fund, World Economic Outlook Database, April 1999).
7 For a discussion of the democratic peace, see Michael E. Brown, Sean M. Lynn-Jones and Steven E. Miller (eds), *Debating the Democratic Peace* (Cambridge, MA: MIT Press, 1996).

Appendix

1 On 9 October 2007, Honduras postponed the signing of a treaty with Cuba until a delimitation issue with Nicaragua could be resolved. Sources: CIA, *The World Factbook 2009 and 2010*, https://www.cia.gov/library/publications/the-world-factbook/; US Department of Defense, *Maritime Claims Reference Manual* 2005, available at http://www.dtic.mil/whs/directives/corres/html/20051m.htm; International Boundary Research Unit, University of Durham online resources, http://www.dur.ac.uk/ibru/resources/; ICJ press releases, available at http://www.icj-cij.org/presscom/index.php?p1=6&p2=1.

Adelphi books are published eight times a year by Routledge Journals, an imprint of Taylor & Francis, 4 Park Square, Milton Park, Abingdon, Oxfordshire OX14 4RN, UK.

A subscription to the institution print edition, ISSN 1944-5571, includes free access for any number of concurrent users across a local area network to the online edition, ISSN 1944-558X. Taylor & Francis has a flexible approach to subscriptions enabling us to match individual libraries' requirements. This journal is available via a traditional institutional subscription (either print with free online access, or online-only at a discount) or as part of the Strategic, Defence and Security Studies subject package or Strategic, Defence and Security Studies full text package. For more information on our sales packages please visit www.tandfonline.com/librarians_pricinginfo_journals.

2012 Annual Adelphi Subscription Rates			
Institution	£525	$924 USD	€777
Individual	£239	$407 USD	€324
Online only	£473	$832 USD	€699

Dollar rates apply to subscribers outside Europe. Euro rates apply to all subscribers in Europe except the UK and the Republic of Ireland where the pound sterling price applies. All subscriptions are payable in advance and all rates include postage. Journals are sent by air to the USA, Canada, Mexico, India, Japan and Australasia. Subscriptions are entered on an annual basis, i.e. January to December. Payment may be made by sterling cheque, dollar cheque, international money order, National Giro, or credit card (Amex, Visa, Mastercard).

For a complete and up-to-date guide to Taylor & Francis journals and books publishing programmes, and details of advertising in our journals, visit our website: http://www.tandfonline.com.

Ordering information:
USA/Canada: Taylor & Francis Inc., Journals Department, 325 Chestnut Street, 8th Floor, Philadelphia, PA 19106, USA. UK/Europe/Rest of World: Routledge Journals, T&F Customer Services, T&F Informa UK Ltd., Sheepen Place, Colchester, Essex, CO3 3LP, UK.

Advertising enquiries to:
USA/Canada: The Advertising Manager, Taylor & Francis Inc., 325 Chestnut Street, 8th Floor, Philadelphia, PA 19106, USA. Tel: +1 (800) 354 1420. Fax: +1 (215) 625 2940. UK/Europe/Rest of World: The Advertising Manager, Routledge Journals, Taylor & Francis, 4 Park Square, Milton Park, Abingdon, Oxfordshire OX14 4RN, UK. Tel: +44 (0) 20 7017 6000. Fax: +44 (0) 20 7017 6336.